to mum and dad

Published by Accent Press Ltd – 2012

ISBN 978190817706

Project Director and Editor
Heather Peacocke

Copy Editors: Hannah Harman, Lucy Hynes, Bridgette Dewar-Mannl

Co-writer: Alison Stokes

Photography:
Robert Partis (robpartis.co.uk), Glenn Dearing (glenndearing.com), John Hooper (johnhooper.net), Edward Mash (edmash.info), Sanjana Modha (korasoi.com), Toby Gee

Front Cover: Toby Gee

Back Cover:
Jean Cazals (jeancazals.net)

Designed by: madamadari.com

Printed and bound in the UK by Butler, Tanner and Dennis, Frome and London

Modern twists on classic dishes

Andy Bates

Star of Street Feasts

Published by Accent Press

contents

introduction

Cooking has taken me on a bizarre yet amazing journey. Who would have thought that childhood baking lessons, and selling pies and tarts in London's East End, would lead me to having my own television series with a worldwide audience on Food Network UK. And enjoying a lot of good food along the way!

Although my life has revolved around food and cooking, I never had any ambition to be a chef – my mission was to eat.

Growing up in a small, rural village in Kent, with my older brother and Mum and Dad, our kitchen was always filled with gorgeous smells of home cooking. Both my parents were Londoners, and meal times in our house were like a typical British menu: shepherd's pies, bangers and mash or roast dinners, with the odd continental influence creeping in such as Mum's legendary lasagne and moussaka.

My brother and I were gannets. We drove my mum mad, ransacking the cupboards and raiding the fridge. And after dinner I would visit my friend's house and his mum would feed me too.

Like many young children, I was curious about cooking. As soon as I heard Mum getting out the scales to make a cake or tart I would be there to help. Mum would stand me on a chair so I could reach the worktop and help weigh out the flour and sugar for her lovely sweetcrust pastry and cakes. As I got older, Mum taught me how to make jam tarts, Christmas mince pies and savouries. These early lessons have stayed with me and I still love making Mum's dishes.

At 16, I left school and went to catering college in Canterbury for three years and then spent six months in France, before moving to London. While gaining experience in restaurants and pubs around the capital, I worked as a runner, then assistant

director, for a TV production company (always gravitating towards the catering truck). During this time I continued to indulge in my love of traditional British food and would often make giant pork pies for my friends' birthdays instead of cakes. Days later they would text saying 'I'm still eating your pie, it's so good.' Then one day as I was walking down London's famous Brick Lane market, taking in the smells of all the spices from the Thai, Indian and Mexican food stalls, it hit me. I was in the centre of London's East End, yet no-one was selling British food. Eureka!

I started my own stall at Brick Lane market, selling the pies that made my friends happy: pork pies, then chicken and ham, rabbit and sage and cheese and onion. I experimented with classic Scotch eggs hiding soft, runny yolk centres, and generously-filled custard and chocolate tarts. At first it was more of a social thing than a proper business. I would spend the days listening to the cricket on the radio and trying to sell my pies. Men doing the rounds with their girlfriends would keep coming back for an update on the cricket. I would give them the cricket score, and they'd buy a pie from me. It was a win-win situation. Friends would come down and sit with me to pass the time. Sometimes my Mum would help out too (and still does to this day – thanks, Mum).

As the word on the street spread, my company, Eat My Pies grew in popularity. My British pie idea was catching on. I set up stalls at other famous London East End food markets: Whitecross Street and Broadway. Riding around London on my old-fashioned delivery bike, I was nicknamed 'The Pie Man'. Living up to the name, I started experimenting with more unusual twists on classic pies, such as chorizo and egg, and black pudding and pear.

My first break came in 2010, when my chicken and ham pie won the Best Pie Award at the British Street Food Awards. It was a proud moment for me to be honoured among the best of Britain's growing movement of street food vendors.

Then I was introduced to Nicole who worked for lifestyle and food entertainment TV channel, Food Network, and was asked to film a couple of pie and Scotch egg recipes for TV "fillers", to plug the gaps between programmes. Looking back, I was nervous and a bit green to the world of TV, even though I had worked behind the camera, but I knew what made a good pie and viewers seemed to like it. So much so that it led to my next break: I was offered my own TV show on Food Network, Street Feasts. During the first series I toured the UK, discovering the best of British street food. In the second series I was off to the USA, discovering the rich clash of cultures and cuisines in the streets of perhaps the most diverse country in the world.

It's been a mind-boggling experience and a privilege, meeting the street food heroes in Britain and the USA, learning about authentic local ingredients and ways of cooking, before heading home to my kitchen full of inspiration for new dishes.

I still wouldn't call myself a chef. I have lots of friends who are, and I am full of admiration for them and the culinary works of art they create. My style of cooking is simple, everyday British comfort food, cooked with love. Nothing too fancy. Just dishes that serve up a great big helping of nostalgia. The biggest compliment is when someone says, 'That pie is just like my mum used to make.' Actually, that's the second biggest compliment. Even better is when someone visits my stall and says, "Wow! I never knew pies and Scotch eggs could taste that good!"

In this book I've taken classic British recipes and given them a new lease of life. You'll find puddings, pies and tarts that will remind you of the good old days but with a modern-day makeover. My knowledge of the street food scene has also inspired me to create new dishes with an international flavour, many of which are included. Whether you're looking to impress your friends with hearty feasts or feed the family with quick and easy suppers, I'm sure you will find something to tempt you. And, once you have succumbed to temptation, you'll come back for more!

pies and pastries

I've often heard it said that there's something about a good pie that makes men go weak at the knees. I agree. I love a pie. Hot pies, cold pies, meaty pies, fruity pies, I love them all. That's why I'm called 'The Pie Man'.

Pies have been around for hundreds and hundreds of years. Today we think of them as a traditional British working-class dish, but it was the Ancient Greeks who first had the idea of wrapping meat in a flour and water paste to cook and preserve it. Later the Romans picked up on the idea bringing pies with them as they invaded Britain, although their pastry was only used to keep the juice in and not eaten. Over time areas of Britain developed their own regional pies such as the Jellied Eel Pie, famous in London's East End, or the Melton Mowbray Pork Pie from central England. Even the Cornish tin miners had their own portable version with the Cornish Pasty.

In America, pies arrived with the British settlers, sparking the development of their own sweeter dishes such as pumpkin pie, which took over to such an extent that the savoury pie was almost forgotten. When I once set up a stall with my pork pies at a food market in Brooklyn, New York, the customers were surprised that the pies were savoury, not sweet.

For me, pies are the ultimate in portable food to eat on the street or take home. There's nothing more satisfying than a pastry parcel of quality meat, fruit or vegetable filling that has been cooked with pride and passion. I hate bland fillings. My pies must burst with freshness and flavour. You only get out of a pie what you put in: the best cuts of meat give the tastiest fillings. And the wonderful thing about a pie is the pastry lid keeps all the moisture and flavours locked away inside while it's cooking, so it should never be dry or dull.

Over the years I've met many producers upholding pie and pasty traditions all over Great Britain, who have shared their secrets of what makes a pie great.

For the best pork pies, use meat from the shoulder or belly and leg. The shoulder and belly gives succulence and the leg adds firmness in each bite. I've experimented too, always looking for new and unexpected flavours to put in a pie, such as chorizo and egg and black pudding and pear.

But my favourite is still my Chicken and Ham Hock Pie, which is here in this chapter, among some of the more creative recipes.

Some people think pastry is complicated to make. I promise hot water crust pastry is easy, and it's the pastry you will need for most of the pies in this section. You simply heat up the fat in a pan and add the flour to make a hot, sticky paste. It's perfect for savoury pies as it holds its shape. Personally, I like the meaty flavour of lard (pig fat) or beef dripping, which gives the dough a heavy, pliable texture, but you can use butter for a vegetarian alternative. Pouring the boiling water over the flour will almost 'scald' the flour, giving a lovely dark colour to the pastry once it is cooked.

hot water crust pastry

For one large pie (20-22cm x 8cm), or several smaller pies

450g plain flour

Pinch of salt

200ml water

170g lard (or butter)

1-2 free range egg yolks, beaten, for brushing

Sift the flour and salt into a bowl and make a well in the centre.

In a saucepan, carefully bring the water and fat to the boil (Caution: lard can scald). As it begins to bubble, start whisking the mixture and continue to heat. Once it reaches a rolling boil, immediately pour the liquid into the flour, beating with a wooden spoon until you get a smooth dough.

Leave the dough to cool for 10 minutes. Before rolling, gently shape into a smooth ball. This will reduce the likelihood of any cracks forming when it is rolled out.

The dough is now ready to use as the recipe directs. Don't forget to brush with egg yolks before and during baking.

Always rest your pastry for about 10 minutes before rolling to allow it to cool a little. This will enable it to fall into your pie tin more easily without splitting.

A versatile pastry for use in pasties and pies, I've used this in my brunch tart and it also works well for some sweet pies and tarts. Always use cold butter, to help create the 'breadcrumb' consistency you need. You can either use a food processor for quick and almost fail-safe pastry or rub the butter and flour together with your finger tips. When making the dough, add a little water at a time. The less liquid used the better, otherwise it makes the pastry hard to handle and causes it to shrink when cooking. Try replacing plain flour by wholemeal flour for a nutty finish. If using wholemeal flour, you may need to add a little more water.

shortcrust pastry

For one large quiche (24-26cm x 4cm) or equivalent

250g plain flour

Pinch of salt

125g cold butter, cubed

5-6 tbsp cold water

1 egg yolk, beaten, to brush pastry case

How much water should I add? Too much water makes the pastry sticky and difficult to handle and it's more likely to be hard once it's baked. Too little water makes the pastry dry and crumbly, and tricky to roll out. The end result will be flaky.

Sift the flour and salt into a bowl.

Place into a food processor, add the butter and blitz until the mixture resembles breadcrumbs, being careful not to over mix. Return the mixture to the bowl. Alternatively, rub the fat into the flour using your fingertips until you get a breadcrumb consistency.

Slowly pour cold water, 1 tablespoon at a time, onto the flour mixture and mix with your fingers until the dough comes together. Cover in cling film and rest in the fridge for 30 minutes until chilled.

Remove dough from fridge and roll out on a lightly floured surface to 5mm thick. Line a 24-26cm x 4cm tart ring with the dough and press the sides in, allowing the excess to fall over the edge.

Place the lined tart ring in the fridge for 20 minutes to firm up. This will ensure the pastry doesn't shrink during cooking.

Preheat the oven to 180°C.

Remove the cooled tart case from the fridge. Line with greaseproof paper and fill with ceramic baking beans (or dried beans, rice) to keep the base's shape during cooking and stop the dough from rising.

Bake blind for 20 minutes. Remove the baking beans and greaseproof paper and return to the oven for 5-8 minutes or until the pastry starts to turn golden brown. Remove from the oven, brush with egg yolk and allow to cool.

Your pastry case is now ready for use. Follow the recipe directions to complete your quiche or tart.

NB: Don't remove the excess pastry until the filling is cooked. Use a sharp knife to trim round the tart ring before serving. This is to ensure your pastry won't shrink and you can pour the filling right to the brim of the tart.

This pastry makes an ideal base for most of my sweet tarts, which you'll find later in the book. It's not that difficult to make as long as you follow the measurements. You can also have fun experimenting with different flavours. I prefer to use fresh vanilla pods in mine, but cinnamon, or virtually all citrus zests (lemon, lime, orange) can also be mixed with the egg just before adding it to the 'breadcrumb' flour mix. You can always keep any leftover pastry. Wrap it tightly in cling film and pop it into the freezer for up to three months until needed.

sweet shortcrust pastry

For one large tart (24-26cm x 4cm tart ring)

225g plain flour, plus extra for dusting

75g icing sugar

Pinch of salt

150g cold butter, grated or cut into cubes

1 vanilla pod (or another flavour of your choice)

1 large free range egg

1 egg yolk, beaten, to brush pastry case

As with shortcrust pastry, chill the pastry between rolling and baking. This will stop the pastry from shrinking, and give an even finish once baked.

Sift the flour, sugar and salt into a bowl.

Place into a food processor, add the butter and blitz until the mixture resembles breadcrumbs. Alternatively, rub the fat into the flour in using your fingertips until you get a breadcrumb consistency.

Cut the vanilla pod in half, scrape out the seeds and beat with an egg in a bowl. Add to the flour mixture and beat (with a wooden spoon or in the food processor) until a ball of pastry forms. Do not over mix. Wrap tightly in cling film and refrigerate for 2 hours.

Preheat the oven to 180°C.

Remove the dough from the fridge and roll out on a lightly floured surface to about 2mm thick. Line a 24-26cm x 4cm tart ring with the dough and press the sides in, allowing the excess to fall over the edge.

Rest the lined tart ring in the fridge for 20 minutes to firm up. This will ensure that the pastry doesn't shrink during cooking. You will have leftover pastry, so wrap in cling film and freeze for another day.

Remove the cooled tart ring from the fridge. Line with greaseproof paper and fill with ceramic baking beans (or rice, dried beans) to keep the base's shape during cooking and stop the dough from rising. Bake blind for about 20 minutes. Remove the baking beans and greaseproof paper and return to the oven for 5-8 minutes or until the pastry starts to turn golden brown. Remove from the oven and brush with egg yolk. Leave to cool.

Your pastry case is now ready for use. Follow the recipe directions to complete your sweet pie or tart.

NB: Don't remove the excess pastry until the filling is cooked. Use a sharp knife to trim round the tart ring before serving. This is to ensure your pastry won't shrink and you can pour the filling right to the brim of the tart.

This pie won the Best Pie Award in the Street Food Awards 2010 and is still my favourite. The ham hock is full of flavour, and the black treacle adds a lovely rich sweetness and depth of colour to the jelly. I've experimented with different seasonings, but lots of pepper and thyme gives the best results.

chicken & ham hock pie

If you're not using a non-stick pie tin be sure to lightly grease the sides and line the bottom of the tin with a disc of greaseproof paper to stop the pastry from sticking.

SERVES 8-10

FOR THE FILLING

2 large ham hocks

1 carrot, peeled and chopped

1 celery stick, chopped

1 medium onion, chopped

1 handful of thyme

1 tsp black treacle

6-8 boneless, skinless chicken thighs

20g softened butter

FOR THE HOT WATER CRUST PASTRY

See page 13

2 free range egg yolks, beaten, for brushing

Place the ham hocks in a large saucepan and cover with cold water. Bring to the boil and skim any scum off the surface.

Reduce heat to a gentle simmer and add the chopped vegetables, a teaspoon of chopped thyme and the black treacle. The treacle will take some of the saltiness out of the ham and give the stock a wonderful rich flavour and colour.

Simmer for 2-3 hours or until the meat is starting to fall off the bones.

Remove the meat from the pan and allow it to cool. Strain the remaining stock into a clean pan and return to the boil until it has reduced by a third, then take the pan off the heat and leave to cool. Place in the fridge until needed. This will become the jelly for the pie later on.

Pick the meat from the ham hock removing any fat and muscle. Flake the meat into a bowl and season with coarse black pepper and the freshly chopped thyme to your taste. Remember this is a cold pie so pepper will really bring out flavour once rested and chilled. Hocks can be very salty so do taste before adding any extra salt.

Next place the chicken between 2 pieces of clingfilm and batter out with a rolling pin to tenderise. Season with salt and pepper.

Preheat the oven to 180°C.

Follow directions for the hot water crust pastry.

Take two thirds of the dough, and on a floured surface, roll it into a circle ½cm thick, large enough to line a 20-22cm x 8cm deep, round, non-stick,

loose bottomed pie/cake tin, and ensure some pastry overlaps the edge.

Place the pastry into the pie tin, carefully pressing into the sides and letting it overhang. Roll the remaining pastry into a circle for the lid. Place on a lined baking tray.

Cover the bottom of the pie with a layer of ham, then a layer of chicken. Repeat this again until the pie is filled. When finished press down the filling so it is tightly packed.

Brush the pie edges with egg wash and place the lid on top. Pinch the lid edge and top pastry edges together with your thumb to crimp the pie and create a seal. Trim the edge with a knife removing any overhanging pastry.

Brush the top of the pie with the beaten egg yolk. Make a hole in the middle of the pastry lid and cook for 1 hour.

Remove from the pie tin and brush the sides and top again with egg yolk before baking for a further 15 minutes. Remove from the oven and leave to cool. Refrigerate for 2-3 hours.

When the pie is cold, fill any holes in the pastry with softened butter so the jelly doesn›t escape. Take the jelly from the fridge, remove the layer of fat from the surface and gently reheat to melt the jelly. Pour the jelly into the round hole in the top of the pastry until the pie is filled. Return to the fridge until the jelly is set.

Serve with condiments and cold pickles.

For this dish I was inspired by Ben Moss, who runs the Parshipship collective of vegan and vegetarian producers in west Wales. The pie is like a terrine encased in pastry, with all the layers of aubergine, courgettes, red onions and red and yellow peppers coming together in a melody of brilliant colours, their flavours still separate but blending at the edges. Separately grilling your own vegetables may seem like a lot of effort, but it's so worth it. And if you're short on time you can always pre-cook the vegetables the day before and store them in the fridge overnight.

mediterranean grilled vegetable pie

SERVES 8-10

FOR THE FILLING

4 red peppers

4 yellow peppers

4 tbsp olive oil

2 large red onions, thinly sliced

2 large courgettes

2 large aubergines

Salt and pepper

1 bunch of thyme

FOR THE HOT WATER CRUST PASTRY (made with butter)

See page 13

2 free range egg yolks, beaten, for brushing

FOR THE JELLY

20g softened butter

1 sachet of vegetarian gelatine

1 litre vegetable stock

First make the vegetable filling. Grill the peppers for 2-3 minutes on each side or until the skin has blackened. When they are all charred, place into a bowl, cover with clingfilm. Allow to cool, then peel off the skin, cut in half, remove stalk and de-seed. You can use shop-bought roasted peppers soaked in olive oil if you prefer.

In a frying pan, heat the 1 tablespoon of olive oil and gently fry the onions for 20 minutes until they start to take on some colour and are soft and sweet. Set to one side.

Thinly slice the courgettes and aubergines lengthways. Place the aubergines in a colander, cover with salt and leave for 15 minutes. Pat dry with a piece of kitchen paper.

In a bowl carefully marinate the courgettes and aubergines in the remaining olive oil, add salt and pepper and the chopped thyme.

Heat a griddle pan and grill the courgettes first, followed by the aubergines, softening the vegetables and colouring on both sides. This may take a while but the results will be worthwhile.

Store the vegetables in separate bowls. These can be prepared a day in advance of making the pie.

Preheat the oven to 180°C.

Follow directions for the hot water crust pastry.

Take two thirds of the dough, and on a floured surface, roll it into a circle ½cm thick, large enough to line a 20-22cm x 8cm deep, round, non-stick, loose bottomed pie/cake tin, and ensure some pastry overlaps the edge.

Place the pastry into the pie tin, carefully pressing into the sides and letting it overhang. Roll the remaining pastry into a circle for the lid. Place on a lined baking tray.

Take the vegetables and begin layering the pie. Start with a layer of courgettes, then season with salt and pepper. Next, do a layer of red peppers, then aubergines, then yellow peppers and finally a layer of onions, seasoning every layer as you build the pie. Repeat this until the pie is filled. When finished press down the filling so it is tightly packed.

Brush the pie edges with egg wash and place the lid on top. Pinch the lid edge and top edges together with your thumb to crimp the pie and create a seal. Trim the edge with a knife so no pastry is hanging over the edge.

Brush the top of the pie with beaten egg yolks. Make a hole in the middle of the pastry lid, place on to a baking tray and cook for 1 hour.

Remove from the pie tin and brush the side and top with egg yolk again before baking for a further 15 minutes. Remove from the oven and leave to cool. Once the pie is cold, refrigerate for 2-3 hours.

To make the jelly, bring the vegetable stock to a simmer. Take off the heat and add one sachet of vegetarian gelatine. Set to one side.

Remove the pie from the fridge. Check for any holes and fill them with softened butter so the jelly filling doesn't escape.

Pour the mixture into the round hole in the top of the pastry until the pie is filled. Cool in the fridge until the jelly is set.

Serve with green salad and a garlic mayonnaise.

For a completely vegetarian pie use butter instead of lard in the pastry and vegetable gelatine.

The origin of this recipe goes back to a time when farm workers in rural Bedfordshire in the east of England would eat a 'clanger' for lunch. Similar to the traditional Cornish pasty, it combines a savoury meat snack at one end and a sweet filling at the other end. There is a long, and largely lost, pre-Victorian English tradition of savoury and sweet foods being on the table at the same time. I love the idea of serving this up for a family dinner with gravy on one end and custard on the other – just mark the pastry at one end to make sure you get the sauces the right way around. For alternative fillings you can use pork and sage on one side with apple and currants on the sweet side, or for a vegetarian version use goat's cheese and red pepper balanced with seasonal berries on the opposite end.

bedfordshire clanger

SERVES 4-6

FOR THE MEAT FILLING

2 tbsp vegetable oil

2 onions, finely chopped

500g beef skirt, chopped into 2cm chunks

400ml beef stock

1 tbsp Worcestershire sauce

Salt and pepper

FOR THE PEAR FILLING

3 ripe pears, peeled, cored and roughly chopped

50g unsalted butter

75g caster sugar

50g prunes, stoned and sliced

FOR THE SUET PASTRY

300g self-raising flour, plus extra for dusting

1 tsp salt

85g shredded beef suet

60g chilled butter, coarsely grated

150ml cold water

1 free range egg, beaten

1 free range egg yolk, beaten, for brushing

First make the meat filling. Heat half the vegetable oil in a large heavy-based frying pan and gently cook the onions for 2-3 minutes until translucent. Remove from the pan.

Heat the pan again over a high heat, add the rest of the vegetable oil, season and add the chopped meat. Cook over a high heat for 3-4 minutes, turning, until evenly browned. Remove the meat from the pan and mix with the onions.

Add the stock and the Worcestershire sauce to the pan. Reduce until you have only 2-3 tablespoons left. Add the meat and onions back to the pan and cook over a high heat until the sauce is just coating the meat. Remove from the heat and leave to cool.

Now make the pear filling. In a saucepan on a medium heat, melt the butter and add the pears and sugar. Cook the pears until they start to break down and reach the consistency of apple sauce. Stir in the prunes and allow to cool.

Preheat the oven to 200°C.

Now make the pastry. Mix the flour, salt, suet and grated butter with your fingers into a fine breadcrumb-like consistency. Add 150ml water and 1 beaten egg and mix to form a dough. Knead for one minute.

Roll the pastry on a floured surface into a large rectangle ½cm thick, roughly 40cm long by 25cm wide. Retain any pastry cut-offs.

Spoon the meat filling onto one half of the rectangle. Using a disk of moulded pastry, separate the rectangle in the centre. Now spoon the pear filling onto the other half. Brush the edge of the long side with beaten egg.

Roll the pastry over into a large sausage roll shape and gently seal the ends. Place on a lightly greased or non-stick baking tray and brush with the other beaten egg. You can mark one end so you don›t mix up the sweet and savoury sections.

Bake for 1 hour or until the pastry is golden.

Serve with gravy for the meat end and custard for the sweet end. A meal in one.

It may sound strange to put black pudding and pear together, but I had black pudding and pickled pear as a starter in a Michelin-starred restaurant and it really worked. So, I thought, why not make it into a pie? Popular in Yorkshire and the north of England, these sausages were first introduced by monks from Europe who called them 'bloodwurst' or 'blood sausage'. In recent years they've fallen out of fashion, perhaps because they're traditionally made with pig's blood (giving the distinctive dark appearance). But chefs are doing great things to put black pudding back on the menu, and I've done my bit with this pie. Instead of pears you could use apple or quince.

black pudding and pear pies

SERVES 4

FOR THE FILLING

400g pork mince

200g black pudding, chopped

1 large pear, diced

1 tbsp chopped fresh sage

1 tsp freshly ground nutmeg

FOR THE HOT WATER CRUST PASTRY

See page 13

1 free range egg yolk, beaten, for brushing

Preheat the oven to 200°C. For the filling, mix all ingredients together and season well. Then divide into 4 x 150g portions.

Make the hot water crust pasty.

Turn the dough onto a floured work surface and knead the dough quickly for a few minutes. Roll the dough out flat, take one of the pie portions and place on the pastry. Cut around the portion leaving enough room for you to fold the pastry around the mix, creating a parcel. Repeat this with the remaining portions.

Roll out the remaining pastry, then stamp out with pastry cutters 4 mini circles for the lids. Brush the lids with beaten egg yolk, then place the pastry on top of the pies and press down to seal. Cut a small hole in the top of each pastry lid and transfer to the oven for 35 minutes, or until the pastry is golden-brown and the meat is completely cooked through.

Remove from the oven and allow to rest.

Serve warm with creamy mash or cold with a green salad.

To get a bright, glossy finish on the pie crust, brush with egg yolk as a glaze before baking.

Pies don't have to be filled with meat to pack a punch in the flavour department, and my cheese and onion pie is full of simple aromas and taste. I prefer to use a mild Cheddar cheese for the filling as it's creamier and doesn't overwhelm the flavour of the onions, but you can also use mature Cheddar, or a mixture, to get the degree of pungency you like best. The finishing touch is the crimp around the edge, created by using your fingers or a fork, to seal the flavours inside the pie.

cheese and onion pie

SERVES 8-10

FOR THE HOT WATER CRUST PASTRY (made with butter)

See page 13

1 free range egg yolk, beaten, for brushing

FOR THE FILLING

50g unsalted butter

2 large onions, peeled and finely chopped

800g Cheddar cheese, grated

2 large eggs

5 tbsp double cream

Sea salt and black pepper

Preheat the oven to 180°C.

Follow directions for the hot water crust pastry.

For the filling, melt the butter in a pan and gently fry the onions on a low heat until soft, then leave to cool.

In a bowl, combine the onions with the grated cheese, eggs, cream and the seasoning, and mix thoroughly with your fingers.

Line a rectangular baking tray (28 x 18 x 5cm) with greaseproof paper. Take two thirds of the pastry and roll it out on a floured surface, large enough to line the base and sides of the tray.

Fold the pastry over a rolling pin and carefully roll out over the tray. Gently press the pastry into the tray base and sides with your fingers.

Tip the cheese and onion mixture into the pastry shell.

Take the remaining pasty and roll to the size of the tin for the pie lid.

Moisten the edges of the pastry with egg yolk then cover with the lid, crimping the edges together carefully.

Brush the lid with egg yolk, make a hole in the middle and bake in the oven for 1 hour until golden brown and the cheese is bubbling from the hole. Allow to cool.

Serve with chutney and green salad.

A seasonal twist on my favourite chicken and ham hock pie, this is a good way to use up those Christmas leftovers. Cranberries and chestnuts add a festive layer of stuffing to the meat.

turkey and ham christmas pie

SERVES 8-10

FOR THE FILLING

1 onion, peeled and finely chopped

30g butter

600g boned weight of turkey thighs, skinned

600g home-cooked ham

Salt and freshly ground black pepper

100g cranberries

200g cooked chestnuts

4 tsp chopped parsley

FOR THE HOT WATER CRUST PASTRY

See page 13

2 free range egg yolks, beaten, for brushing

FOR THE JELLY

20g softened butter

800ml chicken stock

4 gelatine leaves

Make the filling. On a low heat, cook the onion in the butter for 4-5 minutes until soft. Leave to cool.

In a food processor mince a third of the turkey thighs, a third of the ham and a pinch of salt. In a large bowl mix the processed meat with the cooked onions, cranberries, chestnuts and parsley. Season to taste.

Slice the remaining ham into slices roughly 3cm thick. Put the turkey thighs between 2 sheets of clingfilm and batter them out with a rolling pin till roughly the same thickness as the ham.

Preheat the oven to 180°C.

Follow directions for the hot water crust pastry.

Take two thirds of the dough, and on a floured surface, roll it into a circle ½cm thick, large enough to line a 20-22cm x 8cm deep, round, non-stick, loose bottomed pie/cake tin, and ensure some pastry overlaps the edge.

Place the pastry into the pie tin, carefully pressing into the sides and letting it overhang. Roll the remaining pastry into a circle for the lid. Place on a lined baking tray.

Cover the bottom of the pie with a layer of ham and season, then a layer of turkey and season again.

Next add a thick layer of cranberry and chestnut mixture, pushing down firmly. Finish the filling

with a layer of ham and finally a layer of turkey, remembering to season each layer.

Brush the pie edges with egg wash and place the lid on top. Pinch the lid edge and top pastry edges together with your thumb to crimp the pie and create a seal. Trim the edge with a knife removing any overhanging pastry.

Brush the top of the pie with the beaten egg yolks, make a hole in the middle of the pastry lid and cook for 1 hour.

Remove the ring and brush the sides and top again with egg yolk before baking for a further 15 minutes. Remove from the oven and leave to cool. Refrigerate for 2-3 hours.

Now for the jelly. Soak the gelatine leaves in cold water until they soften, then squeeze out any water. Heat about a third of the chicken stock in a saucepan and stir in the gelatine until it has dissolved then stir into the rest of the stock. Leave to cool but do not let it set.

When the pie is cold, fill any holes in the pastry with softened butter so the jelly doesn't escape.

Pour the jelly into the round hole in the top of the pastry until the pie is filled. Return to the fridge until the jelly is set.

Serve with condiments and cold pickles.

With this recipe I decided to take one of my favourite meals – the good old English breakfast - and turn it into a pie... well, more of a quiche-like tart. No full English pie would be complete without that versatile ingredient, the black pudding. The egg, cheese and cream filling binds the bacon and pudding together. Serve with a leaf salad garnish and my home-made tomato ketchup or brown sauce for a great brunch dish.

brunch tart

SERVES 8-10

FOR THE SHORTCRUST PASTRY

See page 14

(Use readymade short crust pastry if you prefer)

FOR THE FILLING

2 tbsp olive oil

1 large onion, finely sliced

150ml double cream

100ml milk

2 eggs, plus 1 egg yolk

A handful of chopped fresh thyme

500g black pudding, skin removed

12 slices of cooked bacon with fat removed

250g Lancashire cheese or strong cheddar

Follow directions for the shortcrust pastry.

Preheat the oven to 160°C.

To make the filling, heat the olive oil in a saucepan and add the onion. Sweat off on a low heat for at least 30 minutes until brown. Set to one side.

Mix the cream, milk, eggs, yolk, then add the onions and thyme.

In a food processor, blend the black pudding till it becomes a pate. Separate into 2 and roll each piece out separately on cling film, enough to cover the pastry base.

Lay one of the black pudding rounds in the pastry then cover with 6 slices of the cooked bacon. Sprinkle with half the cheese.

Next, ladle over with the egg and onion mix. Repeat this process and then cover the quiche with the remaining cheese.

Bake for 40-45 minutes until set, then finish under a hot grill to crisp up the cheese.

Serve warm with green salad.

Chorizo originated in Spain, but the spicy sausage which I first used in this dish was made in the Yorkshire Dales. Chris Wildman is a fifth generation butcher and farmer who breeds Oxford Sandy and Black pedigree pigs to produce the pork for his cured Yorkshire chorizo. You can eat the chorizo on its own, fried or barbecued, but I love the combination of flavours wrapped round the egg in my pie.

chorizo and egg pie

SERVES 8-10

FOR THE FILLING

2 tsp sweet smoked paprika

2 tsp fennel seeds

1 tsp cumin

1 tsp chilli powder

3 tbsp olive oil

1 medium red onion, finely sliced

1 small fennel bulb, finely sliced

2 garlic cloves, crushed

1 red pepper, de-seeded and finely sliced

325g chorizo cooking sausage

530g pork mince

4 large free range eggs, soft boiled and peeled

FOR THE HOT WATER CRUST PASTRY

See page 13

1 free range egg yolk, beaten, for brushing

FOR THE JELLY

485ml chicken stock

3 gelatine leaves

FOR THE GARNISH

Rocket leaves

1 jar roasted red peppers

Store bought garlic mayonnaise

Heat a medium frying pan and dry smoke the spices for 2 minutes, then put in a bowl and leave to one side. In the same pan heat the olive oil and on a medium heat fry the onion and cook for 2 minutes before adding the fennel and garlic. Cook for a further 5 minutes.

Add the red pepper and dry-smoked spices and gently fry for 10 minutes or until they start to take a dark colour. Take off the heat and allow to cool.

Chop the chorizo into roughly 2.5cm cubes and add to the pork mince. Stir in the vegetables, mix thoroughly, season and refrigerate.

Take an egg and chop off each end to maximise the amount of white and yolk used in the pie. Repeat with all remaining eggs. Refrigerate until needed.

Preheat the oven to 180°C.

Follow directions for the hot water crust pastry.

Lightly grease a non-stick loaf tin (30cm x 17.5cm x 7.5cm). Take two thirds of the pastry, leaving the remaining third for a lid and roll out onto a floured surface about ½cm thick and double the size of the loaf tin. You will need a heavy dusting of flour in order to stop the pastry from sticking and make it more manageable.

Gently ease the pastry into the tin making sure it does not break or tear, and ensuring it overlaps the sides.

Take the chorizo and mince mixture and fill the pie one third deep. Place the eggs lengthways down the middle of the loaf tin, making sure the eggs run from end to end.

Continue to gently add filling around the eggs and on top making sure the eggs do not break and the mix is tightly packed in. Brush the pastry edge with egg yolk. This will act as a glue for the lid.

Take the remaining pastry and roll it into a rectangle slightly bigger than the tin. Roll on to the tin and trim the excess pastry then crimp the edges with forefingers and thumbs. Rest for 10 minutes and this will allow the pastry to harden slightly, which will make glazing it with the egg much easier.

Place the filled loaf tin on a baking tray and brush the lid with egg yolk to give a golden finish to the pie. With a knife, make a small hole in the lid to allow air to escape whilst cooking.

Place in the oven for 1 hour or until a rich golden brown. When the pie is cooked, leave it to cool, then refrigerate for 2-3 hours.

To create the jelly, heat the chicken stock in a saucepan and add the gelatine leaves. Stir until the gelatine leaves are completely dissolved. Pour the jelly through the hole in the top of the pie until the pie is full.

Place the pie in the fridge and leave until the jelly is set.

Gently remove the pie from the tin. Serve in slices with rocket, red pepper and garlic mayonnaise.

At my company Eat My Pies, we're always looking for new ideas for fillings to keep our pasties unique and fresh. This recipe was created by my Polish head cook 'Mr Tea'. In this country wild rabbit used to be popular during the war. Nowadays we don't tend to eat it very much, but we should, as it's plentiful, cheap, tasty and the meat is lean and white. What more could you ask of a meat? You can get wild rabbit from a good butcher or game dealer or a friendly farmer. Its gamey flavour works well with sage.

mr tea's rabbit, mushroom and sage pies

MAKES 4

FOR THE FILLING

1 wild rabbit

150g bacon lardons

2 shallots, peeled and finely chopped

2 tbsp butter

175ml white wine

150ml chicken stock

200ml double cream

100g mushrooms

1 carrot, roughly chopped

1 potato, roughly chopped

Bunch of fresh sage, finely chopped

FOR THE HOT WATER CRUST PASTRY

See page 13

1 free range egg yolk, beaten, for brushing

For the filling, divide the rabbit into small portions on the bone and season. Melt half the butter in a large pan, then seal off the rabbit until nicely browned. Set aside.

In the same pan, seal off the bacon until caramelised and set aside with the rabbit. Sweat the shallots off in the remaining butter, add the wine and bring to the boil. Reduce the heat and simmer until the liquid just covers the shallots.

Add the chicken stock, roughly chopped carrot, mushrooms, potato, the rabbit and bacon and return to the boil for about 20 minutes until reduced. Add the double cream and continue to simmer until the sauce has reduced by nearly two thirds, then add a finely chopped bunch of sage and set aside to cool.

Once cooled, take the rabbit out of the stew, take the meat off the bones and return the meat back to the pan. Chill overnight to set.

Preheat the oven to 180°C.

Follow directions for the hot water crust pastry.

Divide the pastry into 4 and shape over a ramekin or jam jar. Place spoonfuls of the filling into the cup-shaped pastry to fill halfway. Squeeze the top together and gently push down, being careful not to break the pastry. Brush with egg yolk and bake for 1 hour.

Serve with cold pickles.

Gumbo is a Creole traditional thick stew made with tomatoes, meat or shellfish. On my travels to New Orleans, local food heroes King Creole and Tambourine Green showed me the best way to make a gumbo, from their stall in the 200-year-old French Market on the banks of the Mississippi River. They taught me that if you want thick sauce then okra is the only way to go. No roux is allowed. The crab claws peeping out of the top are just for garnish, to give these pies wow factor. Serve with a green salad.

gumbo pies

SERVES 4

FOR THE GUMBO STEW

2 red peppers, de-seeded and chopped

1 onion, peeled and diced

3 cloves of garlic, crushed

100g okra, chopped

300g Andouille sausage (or chorizo)

400g tinned tomatoes

1 tsp cayenne

1 tsp paprika

100ml white wine

200g prawns

100g white crab meat

FOR THE HOT WATER CRUST PASTRY

See page 13

Add ½ tsp turmeric to dry ingredients

4 crab claws for garnish

1 free range egg yolk, beaten, for brushing

To make the gumbo stew, first sweat the vegetables with the chorizo for 10 minutes. Add the tomatoes, spices and wine and reduce by half. Finally stir through the prawns and crab. Allow to cool in the fridge overnight until almost set.

Preheat the oven to 180°C.

Follow directions for the hot water crust pastry.

Divide the pastry into 4 and shape over a ramekin or jam jar. Place spoonfuls of the cold gumbo mix into the cup-shaped pastry to fill halfway.

Pinch the top together, leaving enough space for a crab claw and gently push down, being careful not to break the pastry. Place the crab claw, sticking out of the top.

Brush with beaten egg yolk and bake for 1 hour.

Serve with green salad.

food on the go

Street food is an exciting and vibrant way to experience gourmet food on the go. Here in Britain, we are finally catching up with our friends in Asia and America, celebrating street food culture in the way it deserves. The rise in the popularity of festivals, pop-up restaurants, food trucks, and markets in cities and towns around Britain is bringing together innovative chefs and authentic producers with the food-loving public.

During my travels around Britain and the USA, where kerbside cuisine has been thriving since the seventies, I've met many people who are taking street food to a gourmet level. Forget about late night kebab trucks and the greasy aromas wafting from burger and chip carts, and meet the new breed of outdoor vendor determined to serve up quality, fresh, locally sourced produce.

These days some chefs opt work on the street rather than restaurants, serving up what I describe as 'fine dining at a market', but without breaking the bank.

Whitecross and Broadway Markets, where I run my stalls, are at the centre of the street food revival in London. Around the city, traders can be found selling their food from quirky vintage vans and colourful street carts at events like the Zoo Lates festival at London Zoo, Broadway Market in the East End and the Real Food Market on the South Bank. And it's not just happening in London. Almost every city and town in Britain from Scotland to Cornwall has been quick to catch on with its own regular food festival. When you walk about these markets, flavours from around the world collide in a mind-blowing assault on your senses. The delicious smells of organic venison burgers sizzling on grills, huge bubbling pans of Spanish paella, freshly baked waffles and stands of sumptuous looking cakes and sweet treats make it difficult to choose. I could easily eat my way around an entire market.

My personal addition to this street food revolution has been to revive the Scotch egg, one of the most popular snacks on my market stalls. In this chapter I've included recipes for my own classic Scotch eggs, plus some more unusual varieties like the Thai Red Curry Scotch Egg. There are other classic street food recipes, from the traditional Cornish Pasty to the good old American Burger and my modern take on the traditional Po' boy Sandwich from the American Deep South.

scotch eggs

Scotch eggs are the ultimate portable food on the go. They were originally made by exclusive London food store Fortnum and Mason in the 1700s as posh picnic food, but over the years they've been given a bad name, reduced to flavourless, nondescript pieces of breadcrumbed meat and egg. When I started selling classic British food on my market stall, the Scotch egg was one of the first things I made. I wanted to make Scotch eggs that were a million miles away from the ones you can buy in supermarkets and service stations. I wanted them to taste like someone's mum has just made them; and they've proved to be one of the best sellers. Here I've experimented with different flavours, but the principle is the same.

To get the runny yolk, boil the egg for six minutes, then plunge it straight into cold water and into the fridge to stop the cooking process. Once you've wrapped your egg in the meat mixture, do the 'double dip', coating it in egg and breadcrumbs twice, to make sure they are perfectly sealed and no fat is allowed to soak into the meat.

The black pudding Scotch egg is a variation on the basic egg, which uses a mixture of sausage meat and the marmite of the meat world – black pudding.

black pudding scotch eggs

MAKES 4

FOR THE FILLING

4 large free range eggs

200g pork mince

200g black pudding, chopped

Salt and freshly ground black pepper

FOR THE COATING

125g plain flour, seasoned with salt and freshly ground black pepper

4 free range eggs, beaten

400g breadcrumbs

Vegetable oil, for deep frying

variation: manchester egg

Invented by amateur chef and all round good guy Ben Holden. This uses a pickled egg centre and a coating of Japanese Panko breadcrumbs to give a crunchier texture after frying.

Place the eggs, still in their shells, in a pan of boiling water, simmer for 6 minutes. Drain and cool the eggs under cold running water, then peel.

Mix the pork mince with the black pudding in a bowl and season well with salt and freshly ground black pepper.

Divide into four and flatten each out on a piece of cling film into ovals about 12.5cm long and 7.5cm at its widest point.

Place each egg on to a sausage meat oval, then pick the cling film square up by its corners, and use it to wrap the sausage meat around each egg. Make sure the coating is smooth and completely covers the egg.

Prepare a crumbing station by adding flour to a wide bowl. In another bowl, combine the beaten eggs with milk. Put the breadcrumbs on a large plate.

Roll each one first in the flour, then in the beaten egg, making sure it is completely coated. Then roll in the breadcrumbs to completely cover. Repeat the process excluding flour to double-coat.

Heat the oil in a deep fryer to 180°C. Carefully place each Scotch egg into the hot oil and deep-fry for 7-8 minutes until golden and crisp.

Carefully remove from the oil with a slotted spoon and drain on kitchen paper.

Allow to rest for 10 minutes before serving. Serve with a pint of Guinness.

And for non-meat eaters there's the vegetarian Scotch egg, replacing pork mince by a mixture of chickpeas, red kidney beans and cannellini beans spiced with fresh ginger, chilli and coriander, to create a bean burger case for the egg.

vegetarian scotch eggs

SERVES 8

4 large free range eggs

1 x 400g can chickpeas

1 x 400g can red kidney beans

1 x 400g can white cannellini beans

1 tbsp fresh coriander

1 tsp ginger

1 tsp chilli

Salt and freshly ground black pepper

125g plain flour, seasoned with salt and freshly ground black pepper

2 free range eggs, beaten

400g white breadcrumbs

Vegetable oil, for deep frying

Place the eggs, still in their shells, in a pan of boiling water, simmer for 6 minutes. Drain and cool the eggs under cold running water, then peel.

For the filling, drain the canned beans and chickpeas, and rinse thoroughly in cold water. Mash them together, creating a coarse mix. Add the coriander, ginger, chilli and seasoning and mix.

Divide into four 100g portions and flatten each out on a piece of clingfilm, into ovals about 12.5cm long and 7.5cm at its widest point.

Place each egg onto bean mix oval, then pick the cling film square up by its corners, and use it to wrap the mix around each egg. Make sure the coating is smooth and completely covers the egg.

Prepare a crumbing station by adding flour to a wide bowl. In another bowl, combine the beaten eggs with milk. Put the breadcrumbs on a large plate.

Roll each one first in the flour, then in the beaten egg, making sure it is completely coated. Then roll in the breadcrumbs to completely cover. Repeat the process excluding flour to double-coat.

Heat the oil in a deep fryer to 180°C. Carefully place each Scotch egg into the hot oil and deep-fry for 7-8 minutes until golden and crisp.

Carefully remove from the oil with a slotted spoon and drain on kitchen paper.

Allow to rest for 5 minutes before serving.

For this Scotch egg I've taken a smoked haddock and mashed potato fishcake mixture and spiced it up with a little curry powder.

smoked haddock scotch eggs

SERVES 4

4 large free range eggs

200g baked mashed potato
(2 meduim potatoes)

200g undyed smoked
haddock, chopped

100g butter

½ -1 tsp mild curry powder (to
your liking)

1 heaped tsp Chives

White pepper

FOR THE COATING

125g plain flour, seasoned
with salt and freshly ground
black pepper

2 free range eggs, beaten

400g white breadcrumbs

Vegetable oil, for deep frying

Preheat oven to 180°.

Place the eggs, still in their shells, in a pan of boiling water, simmer for 6 minutes. Drain and cool the eggs under cold running water, then peel.

For the filling, bake potatoes for 40-50 minutes until cooked. Scoop out potato and mash.

In a pan, melt the butter, then add the curry powder and heat till it starts to foam. Stir into the mash then add then Haddock, chives & pinch of pepper and mix thoroughly.

Divide into four 100g portions and flatten each out on a piece of clingfilm, into ovals about 12.5cm long and 7.5cm at its widest point.

Place each egg onto bean mix oval, then pick the cling film square up by its corners, and use it to wrap the mix around each egg. Make sure the coating is smooth and completely covers the egg.

Prepare a crumbing station by adding flour to a wide bowl. In another bowl, combine the beaten eggs with milk. Put the breadcrumbs on a large plate.

Roll each one first in the flour, then in the beaten egg, making sure it is completely coated. Then roll in the breadcrumbs to completely cover. Repeat the process excluding flour to double-coat.

Heat the oil in a deep fryer to 180°C. Carefully place each Scotch egg into the hot oil and deep-fry for 5 minutes until golden and crisp.

Carefully remove from the oil with a slotted spoon and drain on kitchen paper.

Allow to rest for 5 minutes before serving. Serve with Mayonnaise.

Thai red curry scotch egg is a spicy alternative created by my friend Ted. As well as ramping up the flavours with some hot curry paste, I've replaced the second coat of breadcrumbs with chopped peanuts to create a satay shell.

thai red curry
scotch eggs

SERVES 4

FOR THE FILLING

4 large free range eggs

350g pork mince

30g Thai red curry paste

3 tbsp fresh coriander, finely chopped

Salt and freshly ground white pepper

FOR THE COATING

115g plain flour, seasoned with salt and freshly ground black pepper

2 free range eggs, beaten

2 tbsp milk

200g natural breadcrumbs

200g peanuts, finely chopped

Vegetable oil, for deep frying

Place the eggs, still in their shells, in a pan of boiling water and simmer for 6 minutes. Drain and cool the eggs under cold running water. When cooled, peel carefully and set aside.

Mix the pork mince with the Thai red curry paste and coriander in a bowl and season with salt and white pepper.

Divide into four and flatten each out on a piece of cling film into ovals about 12.5cm long and 7.5cm at its widest point.

Place each egg on to a sausage meat oval, then pick the cling film square up by its corners, and use it to wrap the sausage meat around each egg. Make sure the coating is smooth and completely covers each egg.

Prepare a crumbing station by adding flour to a wide bowl. In another bowl, combine the beaten eggs with milk. Mix the peanuts with the breadcrumbs on a large plate.

Roll each one first in the flour, then in the beaten egg, making sure it is completely coated. Then finally roll in the breadcrumbs/peanuts to completely cover. Repeat the process excluding flour to double-coat.

Heat the oil in a deep fryer to 180°C. Carefully place each Scotch egg into the hot oil and deep-fry for 7-8 minutes until golden and crisp.

Carefully remove from the oil with a slotted spoon and drain on kitchen paper.

Allow to rest for 10 minutes before serving.

This oddly-named sandwich comes from the American state of Louisiana where, during the 1929 street car strike, poor striking workers nicknamed 'po(or) boys' would be given hot submarine-style rolls filled with fried shrimp, oysters, crab, catfish or crayfish. For my po' boy I've created more of a seafood wrap using fat juicy prawns to make a patty for the centre and a creamy celeriac remoulade topping. The toasted cashew nuts give it that extra crunch. Wrap your po' boy in greaseproof paper to stop things getting messy.

prawn po' boys

SERVES 2

FOR THE CELERIAC REMOULADE

1 tsp mustard

1 tbsp mayonnaise

I tbsp crème fraiche

1 tbsp chives, finely chopped

Salt and pepper

1 celeriac, peeled then julienned using a mandolin

FOR THE PARMESAN CRISPS

50g parmesan

FOR THE FILLING

20g cashew nuts

200g whole prawns, raw and peeled

Pinch cayenne

Zest of 1 lemon

10g panko (Japanese) breadcrumbs

1 focaccia roll

20g butter

10g baby leaf spinach

For the remoulade. In a bowl put the mustard, mayonnaise, crème fraiche, chives, salt and pepper and stir. Add the celeriac to the bowl, mix and put to one side.

For the parmesan crisps, put 4 piles of Parmesan on to a heatproof mat and put them into an oven at 200°C for 5 minutes. Allow to cool and crisp up.

Put a pan on the heat and add the cashew nuts, stirring until toasted. Remove to a board, roughly chop and place into a bowl until needed.

Reserve 6 of the whole prawns and put the remaining amount into a hand blender and add the breadcrumbs, lemon zest, cayenne pepper, salt and pepper. Blitz until it becomes a purée, pour into a bowl then add the remaining 6 whole prawns and fold in.

Put a pan on the heat and pour enough oil to cover ½cm depth. Wet your hands before forming the prawn patty into two oval burger shapes, try to keep the whole prawns in the middle of the patties.

Carefully place in the pan away from you, check after 3 minutes, turn over and cook for a further 3 minutes. Once cooked, carefully remove from the oil with a slotted spoon and drain on kitchen paper.

Take the ends off the focaccia and slice through the middle. Butter the focaccia and place on to a hot griddle until golden.

To serve, put the patty on the bread, then the cheese, some spinach, spoon on some celeriac, sprinkle over some cashew nuts and finally the Parmesan crisps. Using some greaseproof paper, roll it over to become a wrap and twist the ends. Eat immediately.

I used to pile everything on top of my burgers: mushrooms, bacon, cheese, eggs and onions. But as I get older I've grown to appreciate that the key to a great burger is the quality of the mince and melted cheese and condiments is all it needs. For this recipe I've swapped the more common sesame-seed burger bun for a sweet brioche, after tasting Philadelphia burger maestro Matt Feldman's popular breakfast burger. I've used organic minced beef, but you can use lamb, pork or even venison. Serve with tangy home-made ketchup and crunchy fresh onion rings.

double cheese burger

Why rest the batter? It gives the starch molecules in the flour time to absorb the liquid in the batter. This causes them to swell and gives the batter a thicker, more viscous consistency. In addition, any gluten formed during the mixing of the batter gets time to relax, and air bubbles can work their way out, making the texture more delicate rather than chewy.

SERVES 2

400g beef mince

Oil

Salt and pepper

4 slices of Cheddar cheese

2 slices of American burger cheese (Monterey Jack)

FOR THE ONION RINGS

100g plain flour

2 tsp dried yeast

Pinch of salt

150ml lager

2 large onions

Oil for frying

TO SERVE

2 Brioche buns

Tomato ketchup (See page 158 for the recipe)

Mayonnaise

4 gherkins, sliced

Lettuce

Start with the onion rings. Sift the flour, yeast and salt in a bowl. Pour in the lager a bit at a time, whisking until you have a smooth batter. Rest the batter for 30 minutes to 1 hour.

Take the top off the onion and cut thick rings, push the middle out, put on to a tray. Whisk the batter briefly again to ensure there are no lumps. Dust the onions with flour and drop into the batter to coat them.

Preheat the deep fat fryer to 170°C (or a litre of oil in a deep saucepan until a drop of batter crisps up immediately) and then carefully drop the onion rings in one at a time, keeping them moving. After 4-5 minutes, remove them from the fryer and place on a tray covered in kitchen roll. Allow to rest.

Now make the burger patties. Mould four beef patties to the right size and shape for the brioche bun, touching them as little as possible. Oil your hands, not the griddle, and coat the burgers in oil. Place them away from you on to the griddle. Sprinkle with salt and pepper. After 2-3 minutes, turn the patties over and season the other side. Lay 2 slices of cheese over one of the patties and then lay another patty on top, followed by a slice of American burger cheese. Repeat process.

To melt the cheese quickly spray the griddle with a tablespoon of water and then quickly put a saucepan upside down over the burger (in the griddle) to trap the steam. Allow to cook for 1 minute. Take the burgers off the heat and rest. Take a bun, cut in half, brush it with melted butter and put on to the griddle. Toast for a couple of seconds. Repeat with the other bun.

To build the burger, spread mayonnaise on the top half of bun and ketchup on the bottom. Place the patty on the ketchup, followed by the gherkin and lettuce, then cover with the top half of the bun. Repeat the process.

Put the burger on a plate and place some onion rings next to it. Serve alongside a small bowl of homemade ketchup.

american-inspired philly steak pasty

SERVES 4

FOR THE FILLING

1 tbsp olive oil

4 x 150g thick brisket steaks

750ml beef stock

1 tbsp Worcestershire sauce

1-2 large potatoes, peeled and sliced lengthways as thinly as possible

1 onion, peeled, chopped and sweated off

20 thin slices of American or Monterey 'Monty' Jack cheese or other semi-hard cheese

Salt and pepper

FOR THE PASTRY (Andy's Ruff Puff)

400g strong plain flour

1 tsp fine sea salt

300g butter, ice cold

100-150ml cold water

1 egg yolk, beaten

In a deep-based frying pan, heat some olive oil and seal the steaks on all sides. Add the beef stock and Worcestershire sauce, cover and simmer gently for about 2 hours or until the beef is tender. Remove the beef and place on a tray.

Add the sweated-off onions to the stock, bring to the boil and reduce by three quarters until you have a thick onion coating sauce. Return the beef and allow to cool.

To make **Andy's' Ruff Puff'**. Sift the flour and salt into a bowl. Cut the butter into small cubes and add to flour, rub in with your fingertips not mixing everything completely. It's important to see some chunks of butter. Make a well in the centre add two thirds of the water. Mix until it forms a dough, adding more water if needed. Wrap in cling film and rest in your fridge for an hour.

Preheat the oven to 190°C.

Take the dough from the fridge and put on a floured surface. Divide into four and roll each one until you have a rough circle 3mm thick. You will still see parts of the butter in the pastry.

To assemble the pasty, place a slice of potato on one half of the pastry, season with salt and pepper and cover with a layer of cheese. Repeat this three times, then place a quarter of the meat on top and pour over some of the beef gravy, then top with another layer of cheese, remembering to season.

Fold over the pastry with your hands cupping the edge, then cut around it to create a semi-circle. Take a corner of the edge and fold over and pinch. Repeat to form the crimp around the pasty.

Repeat process to make 4 pasties. Brush with egg yolk and put into the oven for 55 minutes. Allow to rest for 15 minutes before eating.

Alec Owen runs Bhangra Burgers, selling fusion curried burgers from a converted 1951 Bedford horse truck. When I caught up with him at a music festival on the outskirts of London, he showed me how to make this great vegan burger which brings together the spicy flavours of garam masala, ginger, chilli and garlic with vegetables. Rough-ground cornfloury polenta binds the patties together. Serve the burger in a wrap with loads of lime pickle, mango chutney and mint raita.

veggie channa masala burger

SERVES 4-6

4 tbsp olive oil

1 tbsp garam masala

1 tbsp chilli, finely chopped

1 thumb-sized piece of ginger root, peeled and finely chopped

6 garlic cloves, peeled and finely chopped

Pinch of salt

1 aubergine, peeled and diced

2 onions, finely chopped

1 small carrot, thinly sliced

400g strained chickpeas

400g garden peas

200-300ml coconut milk

2 handfuls spinach, roughly chopped

2 handfuls polenta

1 tsp granulated sugar

TO SERVE

Flatbreads, salad, roughly chopped coriander, pickles, mango chutney and mint raita

In a pan, heat half the oil and fry off the garam masala and chilli for 2-3 minutes. Add ¾ of the ginger and ¾ of the garlic to the pan. Add a pinch of salt, the aubergine and the onions and fry for further 2-3 minutes. Place the thin slices of carrot, chickpeas and garden peas in the pan, along with the coconut milk and sugar. Bring to the boil and simmer for 5 minutes. Add the remaining ginger and garlic and chopped spinach.

Once the vegetables have softened, add the polenta and coriander. Mix together well so it binds together, you may need to add more polenta to absorb any moisture. Set the mix aside, leaving it to cool and set.

When it has cooled, take a handful of the mixture and press together to form a ball, then flatten down to create a burger patty shape.

In a frying pan, heat the remaining oil, place the burger and fry on each side for 3-5 minutes, or until golden brown.

To serve, take a flatbread and on one half place salad and coriander. On the other half place chilli pickle and mango chutney. Place the patty on top of the salad and spoon on some mint raita over the top. Fold the lid of the flatbread over so the pickles are on top and tuck in the sides to form a wrap.

Recipe courtesy of Alec Owen for Andy Bates Street Feasts.

There's nothing that says grab-and-go food like the Cornish pasty: a hearty meal held together within a pastry fold, it really is the granddaddy of all Food on the Go. The original Cornish pasty was lunch for the thousands of miners who spent their days underground. It had meat at one end, apple at the other, and a thick crimp of pastry around the edge as a handle, to stop the coal dust from their hands getting on the filling. I was taught the traditional pasty-making methods by master farmer Sarah Buscombe of Trescowthick Bakery in Newquay whose family has been making pasties for almost 100 years.

traditional british pasty

MAKES 4

FOR THE PASTRY (Andy's 'Ruff Puff')

400g strong plain flour

1 tsp fine sea salt

300g butter, ice cold

100-150ml cold water

1 egg yolk, beaten

FOR THE FILLING

1 medium swede, peeled, cut into quarters and thinly sliced

1 medium potato, peeled, cut in half and thinly sliced

100g beef mince

400g ribeye, chopped into finger-sized strips

1 medium onion, peeled and finely chopped

Salt and pepper

To make Andy's 'Ruff Puff', sift the flour and salt into a bowl. Cut the butter into 2cm cubes and add to flour. Rub in with your fingertips not mixing everything completely. It's important to see some chunks of butter. Make a well in the centre add two thirds of the water. Mix until it forms a dough, adding more water if needed. Wrap the dough in cling film and rest in the fridge for an hour.

Preheat the oven to 190°C.

Take the dough from the fridge and put on a floured surface. Divide into four and roll each one until you have a rough circle 3mm thick. You will still see parts of the butter in the pastry.

To assemble the pasty, take half of the swede and lay it on one half of the pastry. Repeat with the potato, seasoning every layer. Then take a quarter of the beef and a quarter of the minced beef and lay on top of the vegetables. Season with salt and pepper then add a sprinkle of the onions. Finally add the cheese.

Fold over the pastry with your hands cupping the edge , then cut around it to create a semi-circle. Take a corner of the edge and fold over and pinch. Repeat to form the crimp around the pasty.

Repeat the process to make four pasties. Brush with egg wash and bake for 40 minutes. Allow to rest for 15 minutes before eating.

This recipe combines two classic New York dishes: the iconic street snack the pretzel, and the Waldorf Hotel's famous apple, celery and walnut salad. When buying the pork belly ask the butcher to remove the skin, as this can be fiddly. Once the pork belly has been braised, cut it at an angle to give thicker slices for frying. Pretzels' holes are there so that pretzels can be hung up, but they are also great for filling with Waldorf salad. Finish with a generous drizzles of apple sauce.

braised pork belly and waldorf salad pretzel

SERVES 6

1kg pork belly, de-boned and skin removed (keep the skin)

500ml chicken stock

500ml apple juice

3-4 sprigs of fresh thyme

4 garlic cloves, crushed

1 onion, chopped

FOR THE APPLE PUREE

2 Bramley apples, peeled and diced

50g golden caster sugar

25g butter

FOR THE WALDORF SALAD

3 sticks of celery, chopped into 1cm cubes

6 spring onions, chopped into 1cm chunks

50g wet walnuts

50g Stilton

150g seedless black or red grapes, halved

100g watercress

3 heaped tbsp mayonnaise

3 heaped tbsp crème fraiche

1 tbsp Dijon mustard

Salt and pepper

6 pretzel baps or large rolls

In a pan, seal off the pork belly then transfer to a casserole dish. Cover with stock and apple juice. Add thyme, garlic, onion and seasoning. Cover and place in a preheated oven at 120°C for 3-4 hours or until tender. For the crackling, take two identical non-stick trays, place the pork skin into one of them, season and then place the other tray on top flattening the skin. Cook alongside the pork belly.

Allow the pork belly to cool in the liquid, then remove and place it into a roasting tray. Chill in the fridge overnight with the crackling.

To make the apple puree, cook all the ingredients together gently for 15 minutes then blend to a smooth paste/sauce.

In a bowl mix all the ingredients for the salad. Place in the fridge until needed. Thickly slice the pork belly then pan fry until crispy on both sides.

Slice the pretzel or bread, then place the pork belly slices and Waldorf salad on the bread and spoon over the apple puree and scatter with chunks of crackling to serve.

This dish was originally served at the Coronation lunch of Queen Elizabeth II in 1953. Its creators Constance Spry and Rosemary Hume of the Cordon Bleu Cookery School in London based it on a spicy chicken mayonnaise and curry dish which was prepared for the Silver Jubilee of the Queen's grandfather King George V in 1935. These days this royal dish has largely degenerated to a sad soggy sandwich-filling, but not any more. I confit the chicken in goose fat to give the meat succulence, but if that's a bit over the top for you, just roast or grill it. The flavour of fresh coriander and creamy mayonnaise in the coronation mixture spread onto the double layer of bread and chicken makes this the queen of sandwiches.

coronation chicken sandwich

SERVES 4

1 chicken with legs and breasts removed

530g goose or duck fat

2 tbsp oil

1 medium onion, finely chopped

1 tbsp curry powder

140ml white wine or chicken stock

2 tbsp mayonnaise

Squeeze of lemon

Salt and pepper

1 tbsp creme fraiche

1 tbsp mango chutney

1 tbsp coriander, roughly chopped

60g sultanas

60g toasted flaked almonds

TO ASSEMBLE

8 pieces of thickly sliced bread

½ iceberg lettuce

In a saucepan, confit the chicken legs by submerging them in the goose fat for 1½ hours, or until the chicken is starting to come from the bone. Remove from the pan and rest until cooled. Let the goose fat cool and freeze until needed another day.

When the legs have cooled, remove the meat from the bones and place in a bowl. Discard the bones and skin. For the sauce, heat a pan with the oil and sweat off the onions, without allowing to colour, for five minutes. Add the curry powder and cook for a further three minutes. Pour in the wine/stock and reduce until you have two tablespoons left. Allow to cool.

In a bowl, mix together the remaining sauce ingredients and stir in the chicken leg meat.

Lastly, fold in the flaked almonds and place in the fridge to chill.

In a frying pan, fry the seasoned chicken breasts until cooked and rest. Once rested cut the chicken breasts into slices.

Wash and finely shred the lettuce.

Lay the bread slices on a board and spoon the coronation chicken mix on to the bread.

Cover with lettuce and lay the chicken breast slices on top of the lettuce.

Place another slice of bread on top and cut the sandwich in half.

Once you've built your sandwich, serve and eat it immediately, to avoid the mayonnaise dressing seeping into the bread and making it soggy.

I'll use any excuse to cook with black pudding, and these fritters are a pretty delicious one. I've used hearty authentic black puddings from the Bury Black Pudding Company at the world famous Bury Market in Lancashire, blended to a smooth paté, along with the pork belly from my local butcher, who also happens to be my cousin. The chives give the pork belly a lovely oniony taste and add colour to the dish, and the pears add sweetness. These little balls of joy are perfect to eat on the go.

black pudding, pork belly & pear fritters

MAKES 20 FRITTERS

650g boneless pork belly, skin scored

Salt and pepper

2 tbsp chives, finely chopped

2 tbsp butter

4 Conference pears, peeled, quartered, cored and cut into chunks (keep them in a bowl of water until needed, to prevent browning)

2 tbsp caster sugar

650g good-quality black pudding, peeled, skin discarded and cut into chunks

350g fresh breadcrumbs

125g plain flour

4 eggs, beaten with a dash of milk

200g porridge oats

Vegetable oil for deep frying

Preheat oven to 220°C.

Rub salt over the pork belly skin and then roast skin side up for 30-40 minutes to crisp up into crackling.

Turn the oven down to 110°C and roast for a further 2 hours until very tender.

For the pear sauce. In a saucepan over a medium heat, melt the butter, add the pears and caster sugar and cook until the pears become soft and start to stew. This will take around 25 minutes, if the mixture is still very chunky, mash with a fork to get a smoother consistency. Take off the heat and allow to cool.

Next blend the black pudding in a food processor until mixed but not puréed. Divide the mix into 2 and between 2 sheets of greaseproof paper, roll each mix thinly into rectangles that will fit into an 8 inch x 2 inch rectangle tray. Place in the fridge to set, until needed.

Remove the pork from the oven and rest for 15 minutes. Carefully peel or cut the crackling away from the meat and, if you can resist, put it to one side!

Shred the boneless meat with 2 forks, the meat should resemble string and tear very easily. Season the meat, then add the chopped chives and leftover cooking fat from the pork, mixing thoroughly. In the bowl, roughly divide into 2 and put to one side.

Line the tray with two layers of cling film, then take one sheet of black pudding and lay in the bottom of the tin. Then take half of the pork belly mix and lay on top of the black pudding keeping as level as possible.

Next, spoon on the pear sauce, spreading evenly. Then add the second layer of pork belly and finish off with the final layer of black pudding.

Wrap tightly in cling film with a weight on top and rest in the fridge for 4 hours or overnight.

Unwrap and cut into neat 2 inch squares. You should end up with 20 even squares.

Flour, egg-wash and breadcrumb each cube, then egg-wash again and roll the cubes in porridge oats until completely covered.

Deep fry the cubes at 180°C for 4-5 minutes until crispy. Rest for a few minutes, then serve.

Ceviche is a Latin American seafood salad using raw fish in a citrus marinade which is popular as a starter or side dish. I first tasted it on the streets of Los Angeles at one of the city's best taco stands run by Ricky Pinas. The idea to add the Korean slaw also came from LA where chef Roy Choi, who runs the city's popular Kogi BBQ truck with his friends Mark Manguera and Caroline Shin, opened my eyes to the possibilities of combining Mexican and Korean cooking. All sorts of fish can be used for ceviche, sea bass, halibut, sword fish, scallops, prawns, squid or octopus but I've gone for mackerel. By marinating the fish for several hours, the juices from the lemon and limes pickles it. The Korean flavours are in the chilli and sesame oil coleslaw dressing and the Taco shells brings the dish back to its Mexican roots.

ceviche tacos

SERVES 2

FOR THE CEVICHE

200g mackerel fillets, cut into 1cm pieces

1 medium red onion, finely diced

2 tomatoes, blanched, chopped and seeded

1 chilli, seeded and finely diced

Salt and pepper

Dash of Tabasco or a pinch of cayenne pepper

1 tsp chopped fresh oregano

100ml freshly squeezed lime juice

100ml freshly squeezed lemon juice

FOR THE KOREAN SLAW

½ white cabbage

1 red onion

2 tbsp sesame oil

2 tbsp sesame seeds (toasted)

1 tbsp soy sauce

1 red chilli

TO SERVE

4-6 corn tacos

Soured cream

Hot chilli pepper sauce

Place the fish, onion, tomatoes, chilli, salt, Tabasco and oregano in a non-reactive Pyrex or ceramic casserole dish. Cover with the lime and lemon juice then leave, covered, in the fridge for 1 hour. Stir, making sure more of the fish gets exposed to the acidic lime and lemon juices the leave for a further few hours, giving time for the flavours to blend.

For the slaw, slice the white cabbage into thin strips, along with the red onion. Mix all the ingredients together in a bowl.

Place the tacos side by side and load up with filling then top with soured cream and pepper sauce to taste.

british classics

British food is close to my heart. It's what I grew up with. I'm so proud of our food heritage. In recent years it's been exciting to see the revival of national dishes and regional favourites as more of the UK's top chefs champion our home-grown produce and bring back traditional recipes.

Farmers' markets have grown in popularity in the past decade, as more shoppers bypass supermarkets and buy their ingredients fresh from the people who make it. I have visited markets throughout Britain meeting producers who are passionate about the food they grow on our island.

Each region of the country has its own speciality, and in this chapter I have tracked down people who are upholding traditional food values. At St David's farmers' market in west Wales I sourced ewe's milk cheese for my quiche from local sheep farmers, Caws Celtica, while bakers and event organisers Sarah-Jane Hawkins and Jo Turner of Rosebud Vintage have helped to restore my interest in the very British tradition of afternoon tea with their delicious homemade sponges and sandwiches.

The recipes here are simple, unpretentious and comforting. And of course we couldn't celebrate classic British food without my interpretation of the one dish that is associated everywhere in the world with British Sunday dinners: Roast Beef and Yorkshire Pudding. I serve it sandwich style.

This tasty morsel comes from a time when I worked in a restaurant in Brick Lane, London. My friends and I would turn up for work on a Monday morning knowing there would be goodies in the fridge from Sunday lunchtime, so we'd put together this sandwich. It's worth the effort of making your own crisp, light Yorkshire puddings. Adding horseradish to the crème fraîche gives the sandwich a fresh, fiery bite.

roast beef yorkshire puddings

SERVES 8

FOR THE YORKSHIRE PUDDINGS

250g plain flour, plus extra for the onion rings

4 free range eggs

550ml whole milk

Oil for drizzling

FOR THE ROAST BEEF FILLING

1 onion, thinly sliced into rings

Oil for deep-frying

200g mixed rocket, watercress and baby spinach salad or other similar leaves

8 tsp French dressing (a drizzle for each serving)

400g ready-roasted rare beef, thickly sliced

4 tsp fresh horseradish, grated or 6 tsp creamed horseradish

Bunch of fresh chives

300ml crème fraiche

Salt and pepper

To make the Yorkshire puddings, sift the flour and add a pinch of salt.

Whisk the eggs and milk together, then slowly whisk into the flour to make the batter. Leave to rest overnight in the fridge.

Once rested, whisk the batter briefly and bring to room temperature. Preheat the oven to 220°C. Drizzle a little oil into 8 holes of a 12-hole muffin tin and heat in the oven until smoking. Pour in the batter and cook for 35 minutes until risen and golden brown. Do not open the oven door when they're cooking.

For the onion rings, dust the onion slices in flour and then deep-fry until golden brown.

Slice each Yorkshire in half (not all the way!) and open like a bun. In a bowl gently mix the salad and dressing together, then fill each Yorkshire with salad. Season the slices of beef and lay 2 pieces on each serving.

Mix the grated or creamed horseradish, chives and crème fraiche together and spoon a large tbsp over the beef, before sprinkling with onion rings. Repeat for each Yorkshire.

It wouldn't be a recipe book without the author's version of the simple roast chicken. Whenever I invite a group of friends for supper, I love to put a whole roast chicken in the centre of the table and let them dig in. Coating the chicken in salt and pepper, and stuffing it with garlic and lemon enhances the natural flavours of the chicken. Serve it as part of your Sunday lunch, or even better try it sliced with home-made mayonnaise, iceberg lettuce and crusty French stick for the most pleasurable food in the world.

roast chicken

SERVES 4

FOR THE CHICKEN

4 whole garlic bulbs unpeeled

1 lemon

1 medium, free range chicken

Bunch of fresh tarragon

Olive oil

Salt and pepper

FOR THE MAYONNAISE

1 egg yolk

2 tsp lemon juice

Pinch of salt

250ml rapeseed oil

TO SERVE

1 Iceberg lettuce, roughly sliced

Crusty French stick

Preheat the oven to 220°C. Split one of the garlic bulbs and the whole lemon horizontally and place in the cavity of the chicken, alternating with some of the tarragon to spread the flavour.

Take the remaining garlic bulbs and wrap in kitchen foil. Place the chicken and the foil-wrapped bulbs of garlic in a roasting tray. Rub the chicken with olive oil and season well with sea salt and ground black pepper.

Place in the oven for 20 minutes. After 20 minutes reduce the temperature to 190°C and continue to cook for a further 40-45 minutes. To check that the chicken is cooked, use a knife to pierce the skin around the wing – the juices should run clear.

Remove from the oven, loosely place some kitchen foil over the baking tray and rest for 1 hour.

Whilst the chicken is resting, place the egg yolk, lemon juice and salt in a medium-sized bowl. Add a few drops of oil and whisk together. Slowly add the remaining oil in a thin stream until you have a thick mayonnaise.

Put the garlic bulbs back in the oven for 5 minutes to warm through.

Serve the chicken with the roasted garlic, mayonnaise, Iceberg lettuce and fresh crusty bread.

The best part of the Sunday lunch is roast potato. Get it right and your friends and family will be eating out of your hand. There are several potatoes you can use. Desiree and King Edward both give great roasties, but I prefer Maris Piper, as the waxy, floury texture stays firm and crispy when roasted in goose fat. There are several options for the roasting fat: olive oil is healthier, butter is creamier and will give a golden glow to the spuds, but good goose or duck fat is really rich and indulgent. After parboiling the spuds, give them a good shake to make the edges fluffy and perfect for roasting to delicious crispness.

roast potatoes

SERVES 6

250ml goose fat

1 kg floury potatoes, such as Maris Piper, peeled

Maldon sea salt

Place the goose fat in a roasting tray and put in the oven preheated to 200°C.

Place the potatoes in a large pan of salted water, bring to the boil and cook for 7-8 minutes, until they just slide off a knife when inserted into the centre of the potato. Drain in a colander, shaking the colander to rough up the potatoes a little.

Carefully put the potatoes into the baking tray turning each one with a spoon so as to cover all sides with the goose fat and return to the oven. Roast for 1 hour until golden. Sprinkle with sea salt and serve.

My Mum's parents come from the East End of London and and this recipe always reminds me of times as a kid, visiting my Nan, and she would serve us minced beef with boiled potatoes. It's funny that few people seem to serve plain old boiled potatoes these days, so this is my tribute using new potatoes. With a dash of Worcestershire sauce, this is an easy, tasty dish for a cold winter's night.

good old fashioned mince with new potatoes

SERVES 4

FOR THE MINCE AND ONIONS

1 tbsp olive oil

500g good-quality beef mince

1 onion, finely diced

3 garlic cloves, crushed

150ml Worcestershire sauce

1 tbsp chopped thyme

500ml chicken stock

Salt and pepper

FOR THE NEW POTATOES

650g boiled new potatoes

Bunch flat-leaf parsley, chopped

25g butter

First place the new potatoes in cold water and bring to the boil with a little salt. Cook until tender, then refresh under cold water and set aside.

In a large, heavy-based frying pan, heat olive oil then brown off the beef mince in batches, making sure not to overload the pan with mince. Once browned, place in a sieve to drain the excess fat off and set aside.

Add the onions and garlic to the same pan then sauté them until nicely softened, adding a little olive oil if necessary. Return the browned mince to the pan and mix together.

Once well mixed, deglaze the pan with the Worcestershire sauce, add the chopped thyme, season with salt and pepper and reduce until sticky.

Add the chicken stock and reduce until you have a nice thick sauce. Serve with the cooked new potatoes garnished with chopped parsley and butter.

This brings back memories of school dinners, but in a good way! I was a gannet when I was a kid and ate everything that was put in front of me, but Spotted Dick was one of my favourite desserts. This steamed suet and dried fruit pudding has been around since the 1850s. The word 'spotted' comes from the currants, and some say that 'Dick' comes from the word dough, but there are probably other theories. I love the mix of the hot pudding served with cold ice cream or custard.

spotted dick

SERVES 6-8

2 tbsp brandy

150g currants

25g butter, softened (for greasing)

350g plain flour

2 tbsp baking powder

75g caster sugar

150g shredded suet

25g butter, melted

Zest and juice 2 lemons

1 egg

150ml whole milk

150ml double cream

Custard or cream to serve

Warm the brandy until it is just simmering and throw in the currants. Remove from the heat and allow to infuse for at least 30 minutes.

Grease a piece of greaseproof paper, measuring about 60cm square, with softened butter.

Mix the flour, baking powder and caster sugar together in a large bowl. Stir in the currants (drain any liquid off and reserve) and suet. Add the melted butter, then stir in the lemon juice and zest and egg.

Stir the reserved juice from the currants with the milk and cream and then add to the mix in the bowl, slowly stirring until you reach a dropping consistency (you may not need to use all of it).

Spoon the mixture on to the greaseproof paper square, then roll it up into a sausage shape about 6cm in diameter. Don't roll it too tightly, otherwise the mixture will not be able to rise sufficiently and will be heavy rather than light when cooked.

Tie at the ends with some string and place the pudding in a hot steamer fitted with a lid, over steaming water. Cover and steam for 1¼ hours until cooked. Check the bottom of the steamer from time to time and make sure you keep it topped up with hot water.

Remove the pudding from the steamer and allow to rest for five minutes. Unwrap and serve with custard or cream.

For centuries, custard and tarts have gone together. Some say that even the name custard comes from the old French word 'croustade' meaning pie. Food trends come and go, but the custard tart has not changed much since the egg, cream and milk-filled sweet pastry dish served at King Henry IV's coronation in the 14th century. When rolling out the sweet crust pastry, try to keep it cold, if possible using a cold surface in the kitchen, to avoid it sticking. Sieve any lumps out of the custard before pouring it into the baked case. Freshly-grated nutmeg is the finishing touch for this simple classic.

custard tart

SERVES 8-10

FOR THE SWEET SHORTCRUST PASTRY

See page 16

FOR THE CUSTARD FILLING

10 free range egg yolks

120g caster sugar

600ml single cream

3 tbsp nutmeg, freshly grated

Follow directions for the sweet crust pastry.

Preheat oven to 130°C.

For the tart filling, whisk together the egg yolks and sugar until the sugar has dissolved. Add the cream and mix well. Pass the mixture through a fine sieve into a bowl or a jug. Set to one side

Fill the pastry case with the custard. Carefully place in the middle of the oven and bake for 30-40 minutes or until the custard appears set but not too firm. Remove from the oven and cover the surface liberally with grated nutmeg.

Allow to cool to room temperature before serving with crème fraiche.

This is one of my mum's favourite bakes, a pastry base with a layer of jam and a sponge and almond filling. It's a British classic, invented more than 100 years ago in the town of Bakewell, Derbyshire. But my mum's version comes from my Aunty Anita. When I was younger Mum would always make one when guests came to dinner, but my brother and I would get into trouble for eating it before the visitors arrived.

mum's bakewell tart

SERVES 8-10

150g butter

150g ground almonds

150g caster sugar

75g self raising flour

1 tsp baking powder

3 whole eggs, plus 1 egg yolk

1 tsp almond essence

1 grated rind of lemon

350g raspberry jam

FOR THE SHORTCRUST PASTRY:

See page 14

Follow directions for the shortcrust pastry.

Preheat oven to 180°C.

Spread raspberry jam across the base of the pastry shell.

To make the filling, cream the sugar and butter in a bowl until white and fluffy. Add ground almonds, eggs, self raising flour, almond essence, baking powder and lemon rind.

Pour into pastry case and bake for 25-30 minutes. After 15 minutes scatter flaked almonds over the top and return to the oven for a further 12-15 minutes.

Serve with a dollop of cream.

Why call cheese on toast 'rarebit'? Well, the story goes that hundreds of years ago only the rich landowners in Wales ate such delicacies as rabbit – for the poor people it was bread and cheese, which they called 'rabbit' as a joke. The name has stuck and now it's a popular snack. The egg yolks give this dish richness, while the mustard and Worcestershire sauce add a spicy kick to the cheese.

welsh rarebit (rabbit)

SERVES 10 PORTIONS

100g butter

100g plain flour

500ml ale

500g strong Cheddar, grated

4 tsp English mustard

4 tbsp Worcestershire sauce

black pepper

2 egg yolks

Crusty loaf of bread

In a small saucepan melt the butter then add the flour, stirring to make a roux paste. Cook for a couple of minutes, stirring to prevent it from burning.

Warm the beer in a small pan, then stir it into the roux by degrees, until you have a thick but smooth sauce.

Add the grated cheese and stir until melted. You should now have a thick paste.

Mix in the mustard and Worcestershire sauce and season well with black pepper. Remove from heat, add egg yolk and mix.

Spread onto slices of crusty bread and pop under the grill for a few minutes to heat through.

If you have any leftover mix, freeze into portions and use when you need a quick snack.

The chilli, cumin and cayenne gives this pie a fiery filling as hot as any dragon's breath. The idea first came from my cousin Shaun, a butcher in Essex, who sells a Dragon's spice pie mix. My version is a variation on a pork pie with loads of spice and leeks for Welshness.

pork and leek welsh dragon pie

SERVES 4

FOR THE FILLING

500g free range pork mince (mix of shoulder and belly)

500g leeks, washed and sliced

50g butter

1 tsp cumin

1 tsp cayenne pepper

Salt and pepper

FOR THE HOT WATER CRUST PASTRY

See page 13

1 free range egg yolk, beaten, for brushing

First make the filling. In a saucepan, melt the butter and sweat the leeks without browning for five minutes on a medium heat until soft and buttery. Add the cumin and cayenne pepper and cook for a further five minutes. Set to one side.

Put the pork mince and leeks in a bowl and season with salt and pepper. Mix well and then divide into four balls. Cover with cling film and put into the fridge until needed.

Follow directions for the hot water crust pastry. Once made, divide the pastry into four portions and leave for 10 minutes to cool.

Lightly grease four oval pie rings (13.5cm x 10cm). Place them on a baking tray covered in greaseproof paper.

Pre-heat the oven to 180°C.

Take two thirds of each portion of pastry and roll on a lightly floured surface until it is large enough to line the oval pie dish and overlap the edge. Place the pastry into the pie dish, carefully pressing into the corners, allowing the pastry to overhang. Roll the remaining pastry into an oval for the lid. Repeat this process with the remaining portions of dough.

Fill each oval tin with the pork filling. Brush the pie edges with egg wash and place the lid on top. Pinch the lid edge and the top of the pastry edges together with your thumb to crimp the pie and create a seal. Trim the edge with a knife so no pastry is hanging over the edge. Repeat for each pie.

Brush the top of each pie with beaten egg yolk, make a hole in the middle of the pastry lid and cook for one hour.

Remove from the oven and allow to rest for 10 minutes. Serve warm (or cold if you prefer).

*Note: this pie contains no dragons.

Christmas wouldn't be the same without a plate of sweet mince pies to share with friends and family. Foreigners are often confused at the idea of a minced fruit pie. Victorian bakers would have put actual meat in with the spices and fruit but now the 'meat' is made of suet, raisins, currants, sultanas, nuts and mixed fruit peel with festive spices cinnamon, cloves and nutmeg, and maybe a dash of brandy. Use ready-made puff pastry and good quality fruit mincemeat for a quick and easy Christmas treat that tastes and looks so much better than the shop-bought versions. Serve them warm with plenty of pouring cream, ice cream, custard, or, for a really wicked combination, brandy butter.

christmas fruit mince pies

MAKES 20

FOR THE PASTRY

1 x 500g pack of ready-made puff pastry

FOR THE FILLING

450g good quality Christmas mincemeat

55g caster sugar

4 egg yolks, beaten for brushing

Preheat the oven to 200°C.

Roll out the pastry until it is 2mm thick. Stamp out 10cm x 7cm rounds with a pastry cutter and put in the base of a baking tray lined with greaseproof paper.

Fill each case with 2 tsp mincemeat and brush the edges with a little egg wash.

Stamp out 10cm x 7cm in rounds for the lids and put on top of the mincemeat, sealing to the edges of the bases. Cut with a fluted 6cm pastry cutter for the finished shape. Brush the egg wash over the pies.

Bake in the oven for 20 minutes until golden brown. Sprinkle with sugar and serve warm or cool.

When I first started selling my food at market, I wanted everything to be traditional and British. I had a photo of the Queen hanging on the stall, but one dish that was missing was the classic Victoria sponge. One afternoon I was at my friends Amber and Dave's wedding reception and was served afternoon tea on vintage china. I'm not a huge cake fan, but I couldn't believe how good the Victoria Sponge tasted. I asked bakers Sarah-Jane Hawkins and Jo Turner, who run Rosebud Vintage Tea, if they would share the recipe. It is by far the best I have ever tasted.

rosebud vintage victoria sponge

SERVES 6-8

FOR VICTORIA SPONGE

225g softened butter

225g caster sugar

4 large eggs

225g self-raising flour

2 level tsp baking powder

2 tbsp milk

2 x 20cm sandwich tins, greased and lined with baking parchment

200g jam (Andy prefers raspberry)

Icing sugar, for dusting

FOR THE BUTTERCREAM FILLING

140g butter softened

280g icing sugar

1-2 tbsp milk

Pre-heat the oven to 180°C.

Measure the butter, sugar, eggs, flour and baking powder into a large bowl and beat until thoroughly blended then add in the milk. Divide the mixture evenly between the tins and level out.

Bake in the preheated oven for about 25 minutes or until well risen and when the tops of the cakes spring back when lightly pressed with a finger. Leave to cool in the tins for a few minutes then turn out, peel off the parchment and finish cooling on a wire rack.

While they are cooling, make your buttercream by beating the butter until soft then gradually add the icing sugar and milk until smooth.

When the cakes are completely cold, sandwich them together with the buttercream and jam. Sprinkle with icing sugar to serve.

Sarah and Jo's tips: Always use the creaming method making sure all your ingredients are fresh and at room temperature with equal measures for each tin. Good beating is the key to a really good sponge.

Many people would say Quiche Lorraine is a French dish, but it's really a kind of savoury custard tart, and custard tarts were popular in medieval England too. I've put a Celtic spin on this dish by using ewes' cheese from Welsh producers Caws Celtic. The mild Lammas is similar to the Italian pecorino, while the Imbolc (named after an ancient Gaelic festival) is a semi-hard cheese like Cheddar, Gruyere or Edam. The ewes' milk makes a more solid cheese than cows' milk, and is perfect for this slice of country to eat at home.

three-cheese quiche with tomato and onion salad

SERVES 6-8

FOR THE SHORTCRUST PASTRY

See page 14

(Use readymade short crust pastry if you prefer)

FOR THE FILLING

20g butter

200g leeks, washed and sliced into ½cm rounds

1 tbsp chopped fresh thyme

150g imbolc cheese (or alternative semi hard cheese)

150g lammas with nettle cheese, grated (or flavoured/herb Italian Pecorino)

3 large free range eggs and one egg yolk

120ml double cream

120ml milk

Salt and pepper

150g lammas sheep cheese (or alternative Pecorino style cheese)

FOR THE SALAD AND MAPLE DRESSING

2 large red onions, sliced

6 beef tomatoes, sliced

Dressing made with 4 parts olive oil to 1 part maple syrup, 1 part balsamic vinegar

Follow directions for the shortcrust pastry.

Preheat the oven to 170°C.

To make the filling, melt the butter in a saucepan on a medium heat then add the sliced leeks and sweat off for 5 minutes. Add thyme and allow to cool.

Cut the imbolc, or alternative semi-hard cheese, into 1cm cubes and sprinkle into the pastry base. Cover with the leeks and then top up with the nettle lammas, or alternative flavoured grated cheese.

Whisk together the eggs and yolk and then whisk in the cream and milk. Season with salt and fresh cracked black pepper. Pour into the pastry case then crumble over the lammas cheese. Bake in the the middle shelf of the oven for 35 minutes or until set. Allow to cool for one hour.

For the salad, layer the sliced onions and beef tomatoes on a large plate. Shake all the vinaigrette ingredients together in an old jam jar until thickened and pour over the onions and tomatoes.

Serve the quiche and salad together.

Whenever I cook this dish it always puts a smile on my face. It's been around for hundreds of years and, along with spotted dick, has one of the oddest names of all British dishes. Some people say it's because the sausages peep out of the batter like toads from their holes, although I can't remember actually seeing a toad doing that. The sausages I use in this version are hand-produced by a butcher in Kirkgate Market in Yorkshire, which have lumps of Cheddar cheese running through the meat. Any gourmet sausage can be used as an alternative. The home-made apple sauce helps give the dish its fresh tanginess. Eat it on the go or serve it with mash.

individual toad-in-the-hole

SERVES 4

FOR THE TOAD-IN-THE-HOLE

125g plain flour

2 free range eggs

225ml whole milk

4 good quality pork sausages

4 tbsp vegetable oil for drizzling

FOR THE APPLE SAUCE

3 Granny Smith apples

50g butter

2 tbsp sugar

2 tbsp water

FOR THE CARAMELISED ONIONS

2 large onions, thinly sliced

50g butter

To make the Yorkshire puddings, sift the flour and add a pinch of salt. In a separate bowl gently beat the eggs then add the milk and mix. Slowly whisk into the flour to make the batter. Leave to rest for at least 30 minutes, or preferably overnight, in the fridge.

Once rested, whisk the batter briefly and bring to room temperature. Preheat the oven to 220°C. Meanwhile, fry the sausages for 5 minutes until they start to colour.

Drizzle a little oil into individual oval pie trays (13cm x 9cm) and heat in the oven until smoking.

Divide the sausages among the trays Pour in the batter mix until three-quarters of the way up the sausages, then cook for 35-40 minutes until risen and golden brown. Do not open the oven door when they're cooking.

Now make the apple sauce. Peel and core the apples, cut into quarters and roughly chop. In a saucepan, heat 50g of butter, then add the apples, water and sugar. Gently cook until you have an apple sauce consistency. Keep warm until needed.

For the caramelised onions, heat 50g butter in a separate pan and gently fry the onions for around 20 minutes until caramelised but not burnt.

Spoon the apple sauce and then the onions on to the toad-in-the-hole and serve by itself or with mashed potato.

feasts with friends

There's nothing I like more than cooking for friends and family. A big table, an enormous dish of hearty food, and a gang of mates who enjoy having a laugh together. There's no better way to spend an evening.

And I don't know about you, but when I invite friends around for a bite to eat, I don't want to spend all my time stressing in the kitchen, I want to be able to relax and have fun too. I don't like to show off with anything too fancy or dish up food on individual plates. It's always a big bowl of something tasty in the centre of the table and a 'get stuck in' attitude.

The dishes in this chapter are the type of food my friends and family enjoy. Some are so simple they can be cooked quickly while you chat. Others need a bit more preparation that can be done the day before and thrown together once guests arrive. My hearty winter Lamb and Ale Stew or Whole Mackerel with Orange, Chilli and Olive Oil hot off a summer barbecue, are both easy to make and look and taste delicious. Let's party!

A stack of spicy coated cheese balls makes a great centre-piece for any party table. Chef Dave Danhi is glamming up the classic cheese on toast with his Grilled Cheese Truck which roams the streets of Hollywood. He gave me the idea for these deep-fried cheesy mouthfuls. The paprika and parmesan flavoured coating gives way to the smooth melted Gouda centre, perfect for dipping in the sweet chilli, apple and tomato jam. A cheddar or mozzarella cheese would also work in the centre.

cheeseballs and chilli jam (bolitas de queso)

MAKES 20

FOR THE CHEESEBALLS

250g Parmesan, finely shredded

1 tbsp cream cheese

1 egg white from a large egg

25g plain flour, plus 25g flour for dredging

Salt and pepper

1 tbsp smoked paprika

100g Gouda cheese, cut into small cubes

Vegetable oil for deep frying

FOR THE CHILLI JAM

250g vine tomatoes

1 large Bramley apple, peeled and chopped

1 tsp sea salt

100g granulated sugar

3 medium-hot red chillies, finely chopped

3 garlic cloves, peeled and finely chopped

75ml cider vinegar

Prepare the dough. Place the shredded cheese, cream cheese, egg white, 25g flour and smoked paprika into a mixing bowl and season. Mix together by hand or using a food processor to make light work of it, until you have a firm dough. Place in the fridge for at least 1 hour to firm.

Separate into 20g balls then place a cube of Gouda cheese into each ball. Roll in the remaining flour and deep fry for 4-5 minutes.

For the chilli jam, preheat the oven to 200°C. Have a large roasting tin or dish to hand. Pierce the top of the tomatoes with the point of a knife, plunge them one by one into boiling water for 10 seconds, then into cold water, peel off the skins, discard the cores and coarsely chop. Combine the chopped tomatoes with all the remaining ingredients in the roasting dish, and place in the oven, uncovered, for 1 hour, stirring towards the end, until reduced considerably.

Serve the cheese balls and chilli jam together.

Terrines look complicated to make, but don't be put off. Simply allow a little time to prepare and cook. The name terrine comes from the earthenware dish originally used to make a pressed meat, vegetable or fruit loaf. The main ingredient for this recipe is ham hock, one of the cheapest cuts you can buy. It's the bit between the pig's trotter and leg and is full of fat and sinew, but when cooked the meat falls off and has a strong, distinct flavour which the pepper and herbs enhance.

ham hock terrine

MAKES A 1KG LOAF
(C22CM X 11CM X 7CM)

2 large ham hocks, soaked in water
24 hours

1 pig's trotter

1 tbsp star anise

1 vegetable stock cube

Coarse black pepper

1 tbsp black treacle

1 tbsp capers

5 mini gherkins

A handful parsley

A handful basil

1 tsp English mustard

5 anchovy fillets

½ lemon, juiced

50ml-75ml olive oil

Place the ham hocks and pig's trotter in a large saucepan, cover with water and bring to the boil. Skim the scum off the top, add the star anise, black treacle and vegetable stock and simmer for around 3- 3½ hours or until the meat starts to fall from the bone. Remove from the pan and allow to rest.

When cool enough to handle, pick the meat from the bones with your fingers, throwing away all fat and sinew. Place the shredded meat in a bowl and season with pepper.

Strain the liquid and reduce by half. Allow to cool.

Blend the remaining ingredients in a food processor until smooth, and then pour in the olive oil until the paste is just dropping from a spoon.

Line a loaf tin with clingfilm, then lay the ham lengthways until you cannot see the bottom. Pour in the green sauce mix then repeat the process in layers until the tin is full. Press firmly on the mix.

Pour in the reduced stock tapping the sides until full. Cover with the overhanging cling film and chill in the fridge overnight.

Serve with toast and home made piccalilli. See page 159.

This dish originated from St Kitts and was taught to me by Dean Cuffey, whom I met at Kirkgate Market in Leeds, Yorkshire, where he sells authentic Caribbean cuisine. There is so much going with all the flavours: the allspice in the Jamaican curry powder gives a distinctive sweetness, and the jerk seasoning on the sweet potato gives a true taste of the Caribbean. Make sure you cook out all the spices to really bring out the flavour.

chicken & mango chutney curry

SERVES 2

2 chicken breasts

4 tsp allspice

2 cloves garlic, crushed

Pinch each of salt and black pepper

6 tbsp olive oil

1 onion, diced

1 carrot, diced

1 potato, diced

2 tbsp Jamaican curry powder

5 tbsp mango chutney

310ml chicken stock

1 sweet potato, peeled and sliced

1 tsp jerk seasoning

TO SERVE

Boiled rice

Slice the chicken and season with 3 teaspoons of the allspice, 1 garlic clove, salt and black pepper and leave to marinate, ideally overnight.

Heat two tablespoons of olive oil in a large pan and fry the chicken until it is golden brown, remove and set to one side.

Pour another tablespoon of oil into the same pan; add the onions, carrot and potato along with the remaining garlic. Leave them to sweat for a few minutes then add the Jamaican curry powder and mango chutney.

Once the vegetables have softened, return the chicken to the pan and add the chicken stock.

Reduce the mixture until you have the desired consistency and remove from the heat.

Coat the sweet potato in oil and heat on a griddle pan for 10-12 minutes. Remove from the heat and sprinkle the remaining allspice and jerk seasoning.

Serve the sweet potato alongside the curry with boiled rice.

RECIPE COURTESY OF DEAN CUFFEY

Recently I've started making this quick and easy canape for parties. Using pre-rolled puff pastry couldn't be simpler, and the chorizo sausage filling gives it a spicy centre. Hot out of the oven, they are guaranteed to be gone in seconds.

mini chorizo sausage rolls

SERVES 10

200g mini cooking chorizo

1 sheet pre rolled puff pastry, cut in half lengthways

1 egg yolk, beaten

1 tbsp fennel seeds

Pre heat oven to 180°C.

Peel the mini chorizos and roll them in your hands to make a sausage shape.

Lay the chorizo lengthways along each piece of pastry, roll and fold the pastry over the chorizo brushing the inside with egg yolk to help seal.

Using a fork seal the edges and trim any excess pastry. Cut into individual rolls and place on a baking tray, lined with greaseproof paper.

Brush with egg yolk and sprinkle with fennel seeds.

Bake for 15-20 minutes or until the pastry is puffed and golden brown. Serve immediately.

I first tasted this dish at a beach party. I don't really remember whose party or where it was, but I'll never forget the taste of the mackerel cooked over an open fire. The fish is poached inside a sealed foil pouch where the fresh chilli, orange zest and juice combine to give it a deliciously spicy, citrus taste. The foil also stops the mackerel from burning on the direct flames. This dish can also be baked in a preheated oven. Serve with buttered new potatoes.

whole mackerel with orange, chilli and olive oil

SERVES 4

4 whole mackerel, gutted and cleaned

4 red chillies

Zest and juice of 2 oranges

4 sprigs of rosemary

Drizzle of olive oil

Salt and pepper

Warm up BBQ or preheat oven to 200°C.

Place 1 fish on a piece of tin foil large enough to shape into a sealed bag. Chop 1 chilli and place around the fish then add zest and juice of half an orange, rosemary and drizzle with oil. Season to taste with salt and pepper.

Seal tin foil to create a bag. Repeat for all fish.

Place on BBQ or cook in the oven for about 15 minutes.

One of my favourites, I was first cooked this dish by Phil and Matt, a couple of divers who run the Cornish Mussel Shack at Truro Farmers' Market in Cornwall. They dive in the River Fal, hand-picking mussels from the bottom of boats and pontoons. I had a James Bond moment when they handed me a wetsuit and took me diving. The mussels they pick are the biggest and fattest I've ever seen because they are underwater 24/7 and feed constantly. You don't have to go to such extreme lengths to source your ingredients though: a trip to your friendly local fishmonger will do the job.

mussels with cornish cream sauce and caribbean sauce

SERVES 4-6

2kg mussels

FOR THE CORNISH CREAM SAUCE

1 onion, sliced

130g butter

500ml Cornish cider or any medium dry, preferably oak aged cider

590ml double cream

FOR THE CARIBBEAN STYLE SAUCE

3 tbsp fresh root ginger, finely chopped

1 red pepper, sliced

5 spring onions, sliced

1 tbsp allspice seeds, roasted and ground

1 chilli, finely chopped

Pinch of coriander leaves, finely chopped

Zest of 1 lime, grated

1 x 400ml tin coconut milk

Seeds from 1 pomegranate, to garnish

To make the Cornish cream sauce, slice the onion and place into a pre-heated pan with the butter and cook on a low heat for 30 minutes. Add the cider to the onions, then allow to heat up before adding the double cream.

Leave the sauce on the heat to reduce, until it reaches a desired consistency.

To make the Caribbean style sauce, place the finely chopped ginger into a preheated pan and fry with the pepper, spring onions, roasted allspice seeds, chilli and coriander. Add the grated lime zest to the pan, along with the coconut milk and warm through.

To cook the mussels, bring the Cornish cream sauce and Carribean sauce to the boil, add half the mussels to each sauce and cook for 3 minutes. Discard any mussels that stay closed.

Sprinkle pomegranate seeds over the mussels in the Carribean sauce before serving.

Serve with crusty bread or crispy French fries.

RECIPE COURTESY OF MATT VERNON, THE CORNISH MUSSEL SHACK

I couldn't write a cookery book without including one recipe for stew. Neck of lamb is a really underrated cut of meat which can be tough and fattier than other joints. It's also cheaper, and as long as you trim off any excess fat, it's perfect. When slow-cooked in a stew it becomes really tender. Serve with herby dumplings for a great winter feast.

lamb and ale stew

SERVES 6

FOR THE STEW

3-4 tbsp olive oil

1 kg neck of lamb, diced into large chunks

2 onions, roughly chopped

2 carrots, diced

3 celery stalks

3 cloves of garlic, thinly sliced

1 tbsp flour

500ml real ale

300ml chicken stock

FOR THE HERB DUMPLINGS

250g self-raising flour

Pinch of salt

Small bunch of fresh chives

Small bunch of flat-leaf parsley

150ml milk

Pre-heat the oven to 150°C.

First make the stew. In a casserole dish, heat some olive oil, then brown the lamb and set aside. Add a little more oil and put the roughly chopped onions, carrots, celery and thinly sliced garlic into the dish.

When the vegetables are softened (this should take around 5 minutes) add the flour and stir well. Then add the ale and chicken stock and return the lamb to the dish. Put a lid on the dish and cook in the oven for 2 hours.

For the dumplings, place the flour, salt, chives and parsley into a food processor and blitz until the flour takes on a greenish colour. Add the milk and pulse until a ball is formed.

Divide the dough into balls about the size of a boiled sweet and set aside on a floured baking tray.

After 2 hours, add the dumplings to the casserole dish, cover and return the dish to the oven for another hour until the meat is tender and the dumplings are cooked.

Serve with creamy mash.

In the trendy shopping district of Soho, New York, I discovered Moroccan street food hero Yassir Raouli, who has brought the flavours of his home country to Americans with his gourmet Bistro Truck. Moroccans love their lamb, and I was inspired to use it in place of tuna for this classic salad recipe. Sealing the cumin rub onto the meat before popping it in the oven gives it an aromatic, herby crust. For the salad I soft-boil the eggs so the yolk stays runny. Serve with boiled new potatoes.

lamb nicoise

SERVES 2

400g rump of lamb

1 tbsp ground cumin

Salt and pepper

400g new potatoes, gently boiled

2 Baby Gem lettuce hearts, washed, halved and cored

4 large free range eggs, soft boiled and peeled

200g green beans, cooked and halved

1 tbsp capers

10 pitted black olives

8 anchovy fillets

1 red onion, thinly sliced

Handful of basil leaves

FOR THE DRESSING

100ml extra virgin olive oil

30ml red wine vinegar

1 tbsp Dijon mustard

Juice of 1 lemon

Salt and pepper

Preheat the oven to 180°C.

Rub the lamb rump with the cumin and season with salt and pepper. In a pan, seal off the rump on all sides, then transfer to an oven dish and bake for 15-20 minutes, until pink/medium. Allow to rest for 10 minutes.

In the same pan, halve the potatoes and gently fry in the lamb fat until nice and crispy.

Make the dressing, then gently toss the salad leaves in it. On a large plate, assemble the salad by laying the Baby Gem on the plate, quarter the eggs and scatter all the remaining ingredients on top.

Take the lamb, slice it on a board then lay it on top of the salad.

This recipe is by my old flatmate and catering college friend Matt Reuther, chef at the Princess Victoria in Shepherd's Bush. The flavours of the smoked garlic and the spicy chorizo all mingle together in the pan to make this gnocchi a knockout. Thanks Matt!

matt's gnocchi with smoked garlic and chorizo

SERVES 4

750g floury potatoes, such as Desiree (which should make 500g dry mash)

190g strong flour

30g cornflour

Salt and pepper

2 small egg yolks

1 tbsp olive oil

Knob of butter

1 whole bulb roasted smoked garlic

1 small chorizo sausage, sliced

100g fresh peas, blanched

TO SERVE

Freshly grated Parmesan cheese

Pea shoot leaves or wild rocket to garnish

To make the gnocchi, bake the potatoes in the oven at 180°C for about 45 minutes or until tender. Mash them well or use a potato ricer - this bit is important as lumps will be noticeable in the gnocchi, so mash the potatoes thoroughly to get as smooth a texture as possible.

Sprinkle over the strong flour and cornflour, then season with salt and pepper. Using a wooden spoon or your hands, make a small well in the centre of the mixture, add the egg yolks and start to bring together to make a firm dough.

Knead the dough gently for a couple of minutes then roll out into sausages about 1cm thick.

Cut the mashed sausages into pieces 2.5cm long. Roll pieces into balls and use the back of a fork or a wooden gnocchi board to gently roll the balls over.

Cook the gnocchi in a pan of simmering water for a minute or two until they rise to the surface. Scoop them out as they rise, and place them into iced water to stop the cooking process. Drain well.

In a large non-stick frying pan, heat 1 tablespoon olive oil with the butter. Put the gnocchi into the pan and start to fry until they begin to brown slightly, followed by the roasted smoked garlic and chorizo slices. Cook for a further minute or two then add the blanched peas.

To serve, place the gnocchi in a dish and sprinkle over freshly grated Parmesan cheese. Garnish with either pea shoot leaves or wild rocket on top.

Laying on a whole ham for friends and family always elicits oohs and aahs from guests, and it makes a great centrepiece on the dining table, before being promptly devoured. This dish is easy to cook and is always served on Boxing Day in my house with plenty of mashed spud and pickles. If you do happen to have any leftovers, it's great for sandwiches.

maple glazed ham

SERVES 10

1 x 2.3kg boneless cooked ham

5 tbsp maple syrup

5 tbsp wholegrain mustard

160ml cider

1 tsp ground cloves

Salt & pepper

Preheat oven to 180°C.

Using a sharp knife, score the layer of fat on the ham in a criss-cross fashion.

Mix the glaze ingredients together and pour over the ham. Bake for 30 minutes, making sure to baste well every 10 minutes.

Allow to rest for 30 minutes before serving or serve chilled.

What size ham should I buy? The size of ham depends on how many guests will be eating it, what type of ham it is and what else will be served at the meal. For a boneless ham, allow 230g (½ pound) per person when the ham will be the main meat dish. For ham on the bone, allow 340g (¾ pound) per person.

This dish is great for summer barbecues. The marinade for the prawns uses the traditional Thai ingredients of lemongrass, lime, chilli and ginger to give hot, sweet and spicy flavours. Gently bruise the spices with a pestle and mortar to release their intense flavours. Slice green papaya and carrots into thin julienne strips to create a coleslaw-style salad to serve with the prawns. Chicken also goes well with this marinade. Sprinkle with chopped peanuts before serving.

spicy shrimp kebabs and papaya salad

SERVES 4

FOR THE SALAD

1 green papaya, peeled

2 large carrots, peeled

2 Thai red chillies

2.5cm piece fresh root ginger, grated or finely chopped

2 sticks of lemongrass, finely chopped

2 cloves of garlic

2 limes

100g French beans

4 spring onions, sliced on a slant

1 tbsp sesame oil

4 tbsp Pad Thai sauce

3 tbsp rice wine vinegar

4 tbsp soy sauce

2 tbsp fish sauce

10 cherry tomatoes, halved

Handful of fresh coriander, chopped

Handful of small mint leaves

50g dry roasted peanuts

FOR THE SKEWERS

400g chicken, cubed

300g de-veined prawns, whole

If using a mandolin, carefully slice the papaya and the carrots into fine julienne strips or alternatively use a knife. Place them in a large bowl.

In a large pestle and mortar, add the chillies, ginger, lemongrass and garlic and grind to a paste.

Zest the lime and add to the mortar. Cut the beans into 2.5cm pieces and add. Give them a little crush so they get slightly bruised. Add the spring onions, sesame oil, Pad Thai sauce, rice vinegar, soy sauce, fish sauce and the juice of the limes.

Add the ingredients from the mortar to the papaya, carrots and cherry tomatoes.

Chop the coriander and add along with the mint leaves. Put into a serving dish and sprinkle over the roasted nuts.

Place cubed chicken on skewers. Griddle the chicken on the barbecue (or the stove) until cooked through and beautifully charred.

Place whole prawns on skewers. Griddle until cooked through.

My first introduction to Native American cooking came from Sue Vasa, who runs Zea May's Native American Cuisine on the streets of Philadelphia. The staple ingredients of this culture were maize, beans and squash, referred to as the 'Three Sisters' because they grew together. This dish uses one of the 'Sisters', butternut squash, to create a warm hearty meal, which works as a side for chicken or lamb or as a main vegetarian dish. The cinnamon sabayon gives it a classy finish.

roasted butternut squash salad with cinnamon sabayon

SERVES 4

FOR THE ROASTED BUTTERNUT

1 large butternut squash, peeled, de-seeded and cut into large chunks

1 red onion, peeled and cut into large chunks

1 tbsp fresh sage leaves, chopped

2 tbsp fresh rosemary, chopped

50ml olive oil

25ml balsamic vinegar

10 garlic cloves, skin on

Salt and pepper

75g toasted pine nuts

200g feta cheese

200g rocket to serve

FOR THE SABAYON

3 egg yolks

Pinch of sugar

1 tsp water

Pinch of cinnamon

3 tbsp lightly whipped cream

Preheat the oven to 180°C.

In a tray, place the squash, onions, sage and half the rosemary and dress with olive oil and balsamic vinegar, season. Roast in the oven for 40 minutes, shaking occasionally.

In a bowl, dress the garlic cloves with olive oil, salt and pepper and place with the squash. Roast for a further 20 minutes until the squash is roasted and the garlic is sweet and roasted in its skin. Sprinkle the pine nuts, remaining rosemary and break the cheese over. Cover and keep warm until needed.

For the sabayon, whisk the yolks, sugar and water until smooth then add the cinnamon. Over a pan of boiling water, whisk until it doubles in volume. Allow to cool, then fold in whipped cream.

To serve, lay down a bed of rocket, carefully spoon the squash mix onto the plate. Heap over spoonfuls of the sabayon. Use a blow torch to help caramelise the dish, or place it under a grill for a few minutes. Drizzle with extra virgin olive oil before serving.

This is another good outdoor party dish, but make sure you fire up the barbecue well in advance. Lamb rump is a solid cut of meat which should have a layer of fat on top to help enhance its flavour. I get most of my meat from my cousin Shaun, a butcher in Essex. Personally, I think the salt-marsh farmlands around Romney in Kent produce some of the best lamb. The spicy dry rub gives the lamb a tasty crust and is quick and easy to make. Toasting the cumin and coriander seeds releases lovely aromatic flavours into the rub when they are crushed. I like my lamb medium (cooked for at least 15 minutes). Allow it to rest before slicing, and serve with my almond hummus (page 160) and a fresh tomato and parsley salad.

bbq rump of lamb with cumin rub

SERVES 3-4

FOR THE LAMB

500g lamb rump

3 tbsp olive oil

FOR THE DRY RUB

2 tbsp cumin seeds

1 tbsp coriander seeds

1 tsp black peppercorns

½ tsp sweet paprika

1 tsp ground cinnamon

½ tsp mixed spice

3 cloves garlic, crushed

Zest of 1 lemon

1 tsp Maldon sea salt

Warm up BBQ or preheat oven to 200°C.

Toast the cumin seeds and coriander seeds in a dry pan until aromatic. Place the toasted spices and the black peppercorns in a pestle and mortar and roughly crush. Add the remaining ground spices and garlic.

Rub the lamb with olive oil and roll in the spice mixture. Place on a preheated barbecue and cook for around 20-30 minutes or until cooked to your liking. Alternatively, cook in the oven for 30 minutes.

Carve to serve.

Who doesn't love a bag of chips with loads of salt and vinegar and ketchup? Since the first fish-and-chip shops opened in London in the 1860s, we've been eating them. But it was Mike McKinnon of the American Potato Champion in Portland, Oregon, who was the first to serve me chips with gourmet sauces; from pesto mayonnaise and peanut satay to vegan rosemary truffle ketchup. My version is a creamy, rich homemade mayonnaise with plenty of fresh cut basil – great finger food for parties. I've taken the humble potato chip a step further by using a medley of root vegetables including beetroot and parsnip. Drizzle truffle oil on the mayo before serving to add the wow factor.

chips with basil mayo

SERVES 4

FOR THE CHIPS

2 large potatoes, peeled

2 large parsnips, peeled

2 large beetroot, peeled

peanut oil for frying

Sea salt

FOR THE BASIL MAYO

2 large egg yolks

1 tsp white wine vinegar

½ tsp salt

200–280ml rapeseed oil

1 large bunch basil

2 tsp lemon juice

Cut all the vegetables into large strips. Blanch these by frying at 160°C for 6-8 minutes, then drain and chill.

For the mayonnaise, whisk together the egg yolks, white wine vinegar and 1 tsp water. Then slowly pour in the oil whisking continuously until the sauce emulsifies and thickens.

To finish, finely chop some basil (but not too finely or it will go brown) and fold through the mayonnaise with a squeeze of lemon and a touch of salt and pepper.

Fry the vegetables again at 190°C for 2-3 minutes until crispy.

Serve in a bowl next to the mayonnaise.

A feast for any occasion, I thought of this recipe after meeting street hawker Angus Denoon, who sells authentic Indian snacks on the streets of south-west London. It's great barbecue food and dry baking the chicken on a covered barbecue is the next best thing to a tandoor clay oven, which gives the dish its name. If you don't have a covered barbecue, the meat can be grilled. The tomato puree gives the tandoori marinade its rich colour and the giant onion bhajis are bursting with the flavours of fresh cardamom. Serve with a cool, refreshing raita dip.

whole tandoori roast chicken with onion bhajis

SERVES 6-8

1 large (2kg) free range chicken

Handful of salt

FOR THE TANDOORI PASTE

4 tbsp tandoori spice mix

2 tsp garam masala powder

2 garlic cloves, crushed

500ml natural yoghurt

Juice of 1 lemon

1 tbsp tomato puree

FOR THE RAITA

480ml natural yoghurt

1 cucumber, de-seeded and grated or finely chopped

Large handful mint leaves, chopped

Large pinch salt

1 green chilli, de-seeded and finely chopped

FOR THE ONION BHAJIS

4 large onions

4 large Bombay onions or red onions

1 tsp salt

10 cardamom pods

6 tsp ground cumin

5 tsp ground coriander

2 tsp chilli powder

1 tsp turmeric

Bunch of fresh coriander, roughly chopped

180-200g gram flour (chickpea flour)

1 Iceberg lettuce, thinly sliced

2 lemons for garnish

For the chicken, spatchcock and peel off the skin as best you can. With a sharp knife cut incisions into the chicken so the marinade can really absorb. Season chicken with salt.

In a bowl, combine the ingredients for the tandoori paste, then massage into the chicken. Cover with clingfilm in a bowl and leave for 24 hours.

Heat the grill to 220°C.

Line a tray with foil and place the chicken under the grill or barbeque and cook for 45-50 minutes until cooked through. If flesh begins to burn, turn heat down a little.

Leave to rest for 30 minutes.

For the onion bhaji, heat the fryer to 170°C. Slice onions, then salt lightly and leave for 5 minutes until the onions begin to bleed.

In a pestle and mortar, place the cardamom pods and grind, then add the remaining spices. Add the spices, gram flour and chopped coriander to the onions, mix well until you have a dropping consistency. Shape into handful size flat discs or to whatever size you prefer then deep fry for around 7-8 minutes (shorter time if smaller) until golden crispy brown. Repeat until mix is used up.

For the raita, mix together all the ingredients and serve chilled.

On a large serving dish, lay the Iceberg lettuce to create a bed. Place the chicken on top then arrange bhajis around the chicken. Garnish with lemon wedges and coriander.

Serve raita in bowl alongside the chicken, accompanied by naan if required.

easy eats

Whether you're after tasty weekend brunch ideas, or seeking inspiration for a midweek meal, the key is to keep it simple. This chapter is all about easy eats, food that is fresh and filling and makes use of the ingredients in your fridge or freezer, or stuffed in the back of your store cupboard.

Most of the recipes in this section can be made in less than 30 minutes and in one pan, saving time on the washing up. And even though my turkey and ham pie takes a little longer to prepare, it can be made in almost the same time it takes to watch an episode of EastEnders. And the beauty of this dish is that it can be made at the weekend, stored in the freezer, and popped in the oven when required.

Fisherman's Wharf in San Francisco is where Italian fishermen settled to fish Dungeness crab during the gold rush, and Alioto's Crab Stand and Restaurant has been serving traditional crab sandwiches and clam chowder on the wharf since 1925. It gave me the idea for this brunch dish, using brown crab meat mixed with crème fraiche to create a butter to spread on toasted muffins. I've made my own muffins to get that fresh-out-of-the-oven flavour, but you can use ready-made ones if pushed for time.

crab benedict on english muffin

SERVES 4

FOR THE ENGLISH MUFFINS

150g plain flour

100ml warm milk

150ml warm water

25g melted butter, plus extra for greasing

1 tsp salt

1x 7g sachet dried yeast

Use ready-bought English muffins if you prefer

FOR THE HOLLANDAISE

2 egg yolks

50ml white wine vinegar

250g clarified butter (see below) or ghee, melted

A squeeze of lemon juice

Salt and pepper

FOR THE CRAB

200g brown crab meat

2 tbsp crème fraiche

Salt and pepper

A squeeze of lemon juice

400g cooked baby spinach

400g white crab meat

2 tbsp chives, chopped

Pre heat the oven to 150°C.

To make the muffins, whisk the ingredients together in a bowl, cover and leave in a warm place for 1 hour.

Grease the 8cm chef's rings (or pastry cutters) and place into a hot frying pan. After the rings have heated through, spoon in the muffin mix into the rings until it is ¾ full. Cook gently for 3-4 minutes until the mixture looks set on top, turn the muffins over and cook for a further 3-4 minutes.

Place the muffins on a baking sheet and place in the oven to cook through for 5-8 mins. Repeat this process until you have 8 muffins.

To make the hollandaise, whisk the egg yolks and vinegar in a large bowl over a pan of barely simmering water. Whisk the mixture until it has doubled or tripled in size. Take the bowl off the heat and lay on a folded damp cloth, this will stop the bowl moving when whisking. Slowly, in steady streams add the clarified butter, whisking continuously. When the butter is mixed in and emulsified, add the lemon juice and season, then whisk again and keep warm.

Now prepare the crab. In a small saucepan combine the crème fraiche and brown crab. Bring to a simmer then season and add a squeeze of lemon juice.

To serve, take a muffin and spread with brown crab mix. Add a quarter of the spinach and then a quarter of the white crab meat. Pour over the Hollandaise and then finish with another muffin rested on top.

To clarify butter, heat it over a low heat until melted. Skim off any foam and pour the clarified butter from the pan, taking care to leave behind the milk solids.

This filling snack has no diary or animal products, yet still manages to be tasty and light. Instead of the usual eggs and butter I've used olive oil and self-raising flour, which gives the batter a fluffy texture. What I love about this dish is the colours: the orange of butternut squash, the red of pepper and kidney beans, and yellow sweetcorn. It also reminds me of when I was a kid and would watch my Dad flipping pancakes on Shrove Tuesday. If you're making a batch of these pancakes, use greaseproof paper on top of each one when stacking them, to stop them sticking before you fill them.

vegan pancakes

SERVES 6

FOR THE PANCAKES

300g self-raising flour

1 tsp salt

500ml water

50ml olive oil, plus extra for frying

SWEET PAPRIKA VEGETABLE FILLING

1 onion, peeled and diced

3 cloves of garlic, crushed

1 red pepper, diced

1 tsp smoked paprika

300g squash, peeled and diced

400g kidney beans, drained

200g sweetcorn

300ml vegetable stock

Whisk all the ingredients together for the pancakes.

In a large frying pan drizzle some oil and allow to warm through, then pour in some of the pancake batter and swirl it around so it covers the base of the frying pan. Fry for a couple of minutes on either side, until golden brown. Once cooked, place each pancake on a layer of greaseproof paper, cover and set to one side.

For the filling, sweat the onions and garlic until translucent, then add all remaining ingredients into a saucepan, bring to the boil and simmer for 15 minutes until the mixture thickens.

To serve, fold each pancake in half, then in half again and fill the two pockets with the filling.

My friends and I came up with this recipe when we worked in a Tex Mex restaurant in Kent. Everyone working there was English, and every morning we would turn up and find a fridge full of bacon, sausages and mushrooms but no bread. You can imagine the disappointment. This gave me the idea of filling a tortilla with cheese, cooked bacon, sausage and mushroom, folding it over and cooking it like a quesadilla. I topped it with beans instead of salsa and finished it off with a dollop of sour cream. It shouldn't work, but it does!

british breakfast quesadilla

SERVES 2

3 good quality sausages

2 large field mushrooms

4 bacon rashers

4 large flour tortillas

150g Cheddar cheese, grated

4 tbsp soured cream

200g baked beans

2 spring onions, finely chopped

In a large saucepan, fry the sausages, mushrooms and bacon to your preference, then cut into roughly 1cm sized pieces and set aside.

Place one tortilla in the bottom of a large dry sauté or frying pan on a medium heat. Sprinkle with half the cheddar, then the bacon, sausages and mushrooms and sprinkle with the remaining cheese, and then season.

Place another tortilla on top and cook for a few minutes on each side until cheese has melted and the tortillas are nice and crispy.

Turn onto a plate and cut into 8 pieces.

To serve, top with hot baked beans, a large tablespoon of soured cream and finely chopped spring onions.

This is like two supper dishes in one. The fresh chestnut mushroom soup is lovely, but the best bit is the giant crouton. A long toasted slice of French bread, topped with bacon, mushroom and melted cheese. Use it as a spoon to scoop up the soup. Then when all the soup has gone, soaked into the bread, you can polish off the crouton.

mushroom and gruyere soup

SERVES 4

FOR THE SOUP

1 large onion, peeled and diced

2 large potatoes, peeled and diced

400g chestnut mushrooms

1 litre vegetable stock

Salt and pepper

FOR THE CROUTONS

French stick

Pan-fried fresh mushrooms

Diced crispy bacon

100g grated Gruyere

TO SERVE

150ml double cream

Handful of chopped parsley

Place all the ingredients for the soup in a large pan, bring to the boil then simmer for 15 minutes. Blitz with a stick blender. Add the cream, and check the seasoning.

Preheat the grill to 200°C.

To make the croutons, thinly slice a French stick at diagonal angle. Brush with butter on both sides, then grill until toasted and crispy. Set to one side.

Pan fry the mushrooms and bacon then spoon on top of the croutons, cover with cheese and grill.

Pour the soup into warm bowls, drizzle with cream and sprinkle with chopped parsley. Serve with the crouton sitting across the edge of the bowl.

My friend Nick Hatfield does a version of this in his pub using cod, but I opted for the meatier texture of monkfish which works well with the melted cheese topping. As I've added chorizo to the rarebit, I' thought I'd better keep to a Spanish theme with manchego cheese and Spanish lager. But any hard cheese or lager will work too.

monkfish with chorizo welsh rarebit

SERVES 2

2 x 200g monkfish steaks

FOR THE RAREBIT

1 tsp English mustard powder

3 tbsp Spanish lager

30g butter

175g manchego cheese, grated

50g chorizo, cut into 0.5cm cubes

2 egg yolks

4 large tomatoes, sliced

FOR THE DRESSING

2 tbsp olive oil

2 tbsp fresh tarragon, chopped

Juice of 1 lemon

50g clams cooked, out of shells

Preheat oven to 180°C.

To make the rarebit, mix the mustard powder with 1 tablespoon of lager in the bottom of a small pan to make a paste, then stir in the rest of the lager and add the butter. Heat gently to melt the butter, add the cheese and stir to melt, but do not let the mixture boil.

Once smooth, add the chorizo. Allow it to cool to room temperature then beat in the yolks. Place the monkfish on the tray and shape the rarebit to fit over. Place in a preheated oven for 10-15 minutes or until the fish is cooked. If necessary, pop under the grill to brown the rarebit.

In a bowl, mix all the ingredients together for the dressing then add the clams. Arrange the sliced tomatoes on plates, drizzle some dressing over, then top with the monkfish rarebit. Serve immediately.

Rib-eye is one of the more expensive cuts of meat, but it's juicy and succulent and a good main ingredient for this salad. Quick to cook, the internal fat of the steak caramelises on the griddle or frying pan to add a depth of flavour. The dressing takes seconds to whisk together. I find the strong nutty flavour of the blue cheese works well with the sweetness of the pears.

beef, stilton and pear salad

SERVES 2

FOR THE SALAD

Olive oil

2 rib-eye steaks

Salt and pepper

3 pears, peeled and cored

A handful of watercress

Leaves of 1 red and 1 yellow chicory

150g Stilton, crumbled

FOR THE DRESSING

5 tbsp olive oil

1 tbsp wholegrain mustard

1 tsp clear honey

1 lemon

Pour a little olive oil onto your hands and rub this onto the steaks, season each side then put them onto a smoking hot griddle pan or frying pan. Cook the steaks until medium rare, this should take around 3 minutes each side, then set aside to rest.

With a melon baller, ball out the pear and keep in water. It is nicer if the pear balls are different sizes. Sort the watercress and chicory leaves and place on a serving dish.

To make the dressing, simply place the oil, mustard, honey and the juice of half the lemon in a bowl and whisk together. Taste for seasoning and set aside.

Slice the rested ribeye steaks into thin strips and then roll them up and place on top of the watercress and chicory leaves. Crumble the Stilton over and then dot the pear balls around the dish. Dress the dish with the mustard, honey and lemon dressing.

Pearl barley is one of those store cupboard ingredients I never know what to do with. It comes from the part of the barley that has had the bran removed to give it its pearly white colour and is mostly used to thicken soups and stews. In this recipe, I've used it as an alternative to risotto rice using chicken left over from a Sunday roast. Pearl barley has a nuttier taste than standard risotto rice.

chicken and pearl barley risotto

SERVES 2 LARGE PORTIONS, OR 4 AS A STARTER

1 medium onion, finely chopped

3 tbsp olive oil

500g pearl barley

200ml white wine

1 litre chicken stock

50g grated Parmesan cheese

80ml double cream

Salt and pepper

1 cooked roast chicken, meat pulled off the bone and shredded

Place the onion in a large sauté pan with the olive oil. Sweat the onion without colouring until translucent, then add the pearl barley and mix, making sure you coat the pearl barley with the oil in the pan.

Add the wine to the pan and cook on a medium heat until almost all the wine has absorbed. Then add the hot stock a ladleful at a time, waiting for each ladleful to absorb before adding the next. Keep stirring continuously.

Continue this process until the barley is cooked (it should take about 30 minutes) tasting as you go. When cooked, stir in the Parmesan, then the cream and season. Finally, fold through the shredded chicken and serve.

This is a good way to use up the turkey after Christmas. Once you've made the pie, you can put it in the freezer and take it out at a later date to serve with mash or greens.

turkey and leek pie

SERVES 4

75g butter

75g flour

1 litre chicken stock

Handful of chopped fresh thyme

300ml double cream

350g cooked or leftover turkey or chicken

350g sweated-down leeks

Pre-rolled puff pastry (400g pack)

1 egg yolk, beaten, for brushing pastry

Preheat the oven to 190°C.

In a saucepan melt the butter on a medium heat and add the flour, stirring constantly until you have a roux. Cook gently for 3 minutes then slowly add the stock, one ladleful at a time, stirring continuously until you have a lump-free sauce.

On a low heat, simmer the sauce for 10-15 minutes to cook out the flour taste. Add the chopped thyme and double cream and season to taste. Allow to cool.

Place the turkey (or chicken) and leeks in an ovenproof rectangular dish 20cm x 10cm x 5cm, pour over the sauce then roll your pastry over, making sure it overlaps the edges by 1-2cm. Gently press down the edges to seal the pie. Make a hole in the lid to allow steam to escape.

Rest in the fridge for 10 minutes.

Brush with egg yolk and cook in the preheated oven for 35-40 minutes. Serve with mash and greens.

posh bacon sarny with scallops

SERVES 2

2 rashers streaked smoked bacon

2 tbsp maple syrup

4 fresh scallops

1 tbsp olive oil

1 tsp butter

English muffins

FOR THE HOLLANDAISE

3 egg yolks

2 tbsp reduced white wine vinegar

200g melted clarified butter

Squeeze of lemon

To make the hollandaise, blend the egg yolks in a food processor or with a hand mixer for one minute. In a small saucepan, heat the lemon juice and white wine vinegar until they begin to simmer. Remove from the heat.

Switch on the food /hand mixer again and in a slow, steady stream, pour in the lemon and white wine vinegar mixture and blend for a further minute or two.

Gently melt the butter in a small saucepan. Allow it to foam, then switch off the heat. Using the food processor or hand mixer, gradually pour the butter into the egg mixture in a slow steady stream. Blend thoroughly, pour into a jug and set aside.

Bake bacon until crispy, brush with ample syrup and keep warm.

In a heavy bottomed pan heat the oil and pan fry the scallops for one minute on each side, add the butter and squeeze of lemon to the pan. Put scallops with bacon to keep warm.

Cut each English muffin in two and toast.

Arrange on plate and drizzle with Hollandaise.

I love serving up a tasty supper in record time, and this soup is a classic example. In the East End where my Nan lives, on foggy days they used to say 'it's a real pea-souper'. I always thought it was strange but the expression came from the traditional English split pea soup, which was greeny-brown and thick, like London smog in days gone by. The frozen peas give this dish a much more vibrant green colour. You can also use fresh peas for the same effect. Serve with lots of warm, fresh bread.

ham and pea soup

SERVES 8

Knob of butter

1 medium onion, finely chopped

1 garlic clove

2 tbsp flour

1.5l chicken or ham stock

500ml milk

900g frozen peas

Salt and freshly ground black pepper

500g cooked ham, diced into 1-2cm cubes

Crème fraiche

Chopped parsley

In a large saucepan, heat a knob of butter, then sweat the onion and garlic for 5 minutes. Add the flour and cook out for 3 minutes.

Slowly pour in the stock, stirring continuously. Then add the milk. Bring to the boil, add the peas and cook for no more than 5 minutes.

Puree in a blender in batches, filling no more than half full for each batch.

Return the soup to a clean pan, season, add the ham and warm through.

Serve in a bowl with crème fraiche and chopped parsley.

I was taught how to make this popular New England creamy fish stew in San Francisco. It's a lot easier to cook than you might think. For me, it's fisherman's pie turned upside down: a creamy fish broth poured over a bed of mashed potato. The yellow sweetcorn and the clams poking out of their shells make this a supper dish.

chowder and mash

SERVES 4-6

600g smoked haddock, naturally dyed

300ml chicken or fish stock

150ml white wine

200g raw tiger prawns

100g clams in shells, cleaned

200g sweetcorn

200ml double cream

Salt and pepper

25g butter

1 onion, finely chopped

600g mashed potato

¼ tsp nutmeg

2 tsp fresh chives, chopped

In a large frying pan, poach the haddock in the stock and wine for five minutes. Remove the haddock from the pan, put on a tray, cover in foil and keep warm.

Bring the cooking liquid up to the boil and reduce by half. Add the prawns, clams, sweetcorn and half the cream, then season with salt and pepper.

For the mash, heat the butter in a pan and fry off the onions for 2-3 minutes. Add the mashed potato, remaining cream and nutmeg and beat together.

To serve, put a pile of mash on the plate, sit the haddock on top, pour over the sauce then sprinkle with chives.

Purging (cleaning) clams. To avoid getting a mouthful of sand and grit with your clams, it's a good idea to clean or purge them before cooking.

Most shop-bought clams have already been purged, but you can easily do it yourself if required. Rinse the clams under cold water, then place them in a bowl of cold salted water. If you don't like the look of the dark stomach contents coming from the shellfish, add some polenta flour to the water and the clams will feed on this while they're soaking. Leave for about two hours, rinse with cold water and they're ready to cook.

One-pot cooking doesn't get much tastier than this simple sandwich. There are so many of my favourite ingredients in this dish especially the morcillo de bergos – that's a Spanish version of, wait for it, black pudding. Cooking the chicken livers and mushrooms in the same pan brings all the flavours together.

chicken liver and mushroom open sandwich

SERVES 2-4

1 large ciabatta or foccacia

1 garlic clove, halved

Olive oil

Salt

1 morcilla de burgos (Spanish black pudding) or British black pudding

Flour (seasoned with salt and pepper) for dusting the livers

400g chicken livers

125g butter

200g mixed sliced mushrooms (chestnut, shitake, oyster)

2 shallots, finely chopped

1 tbsp fresh tarragon, finely chopped

1 tbsp flat-leaf parsley, finely chopped

Squeeze of lemon juice

Slice the bread lengthways to open up 2 halves (open sandwich). Rub with garlic and lightly drizzle with olive oil. Over a griddle or frying pan, toast the open halves. Lightly sprinkle with salt and keep warm.

Slice the black pudding into 1cm slices and griddle or pan fry until crispy. Place the slices on top of the bread and keep warm.

In a tray sift the flour, season and place the livers in. Shake off any excess flour. In the same pan you used for the black pudding, heat 2 tablespoons of oil and, when smoking, place the livers in one at a time and cook for 1 minute on each side. Remove from the pan, place on a tray and keep warm.

Again, using the same pan, add half the butter and over a high heat fry off the mushrooms until just cooked. Season and add to the livers. Cover with foil and keep warm.

Add the rest of the butter to the pan and gently sweat off the shallots for 5 minutes. Once translucent, return the livers and mushrooms to the pan and heat for 2-3 minutes.

Add the herbs and gently mix through, check for seasoning. Place the bread on plates and spoon the liver and mushroom mix on top.

Drizzle with olive oil and a squeeze of lemon on each one before serving.

puddings and tarts

'What's for pudding?' was a common refrain in our house. Then Mum would appear with one of her home-made tarts or rhubarb crumble sitting in a puddle of custard.

Pudding – or 'pud' – is a very British term for the sweet course at the end of a menu. And I have to admit there's something really reassuring about ending a meal with a bowl of thick, creamy custard, enveloping a hot, steamed sponge.

There are hundreds of variations of sweet puddings, each beginning with the same basic ingredients: milk, sugar, eggs, flour and butter.

Fashionable in Victorian times, the British pud fell out of favour in the early 20th century, following the introduction of fridges, which gave rise to cold desserts like ice cream. Wartime rationing meant ingredients for traditional puds grew scarce, and later the trend for healthy eating relegated them to the food subs bench. But I'm pleased to see real old puddings making a comeback, with leading restaurants now proudly listing them on their menus.

This section features traditional British puddings and tarts, including Apple and Raspberry Crumble, and my own personal favourite and bestseller on my market stall, the Milk Chocolate Tart, which I make with a really thick, deep filling. I've also included a modern variation of traditional bread and butter pudding, and given Derbyshire's classic Bakewell Tart an American twist.

Everyone raves about dark chocolate and the high cocoa content making it far superior, but I just love the smoothness of milk chocolate. And there are lots of people who agree, as this is one of the cornerstones of my business. Use a high-sided tin for a lovely, deep, thick tart. For the finishing touches, dust with cocoa powder and serve with thick cream.

milk chocolate tart

SERVES 8-10

FOR THE SWEET SHORTCRUST PASTRY

See page 16

FOR THE FILLING

450ml single cream

150ml whole milk

600g milk chocolate (minimum 35% cocoa solids), melted

3 free range eggs

Follow directions for the sweet shortcrust pastry.

Preheat the oven to 140°C.

For the filling, bring the cream and milk to the boil and pour over the chocolate and stir until chocolate and cream are mixed. Allow to cool for 5 minutes. Beat the eggs then add to the chocolate and mix well.

Fill the pastry case with the chocolate filling. Carefully place in the middle of the oven and bake for 30-40 minutes or until the filling appears set but with a slight wobble.

Allow to cool to room temperature before serving.

variation: white chocolate and raspberry tart

400g white chocolate, broken into pieces

300ml single cream

60ml whole milk

2 free range eggs

600g fresh raspberries

Icing sugar to dust

Follow the directions above, adjusting the ingredients and quantities.

Once cooked, allow the tart to cool to room temperature, then place in the fridge until completely set.

Before serving, cover with raspberries. Starting from the outside edge, carefully place the raspberries on the tart, working towards the middle. Dust with icing sugar

blueberry bakewell tart with raspberry chantilly cream

An American twist on the classic English tart, served with sweet French whipped cream. This recipe came to me on a visit to Portland, Oregon, where I stopped off at The Pie Stop and tried the most popular pie filled with fat, delicious, local blueberries. I love using fresh berries in pies. Blueberries give this tart a lovely spotted effect, while tangy raspberries enhance the cream.

SERVES 8

FOR THE SHORT CRUST PASTRY

See page 14

FOR THE FILLING

100g butter

225g golden caster sugar

3 eggs, beaten, plus 1 egg yolk

50g plain flour

350g wild blueberry jam (1 jar)

100g blueberries

80g ground almonds

50g toasted almonds for garnish

FOR THE CHANTILLY CREAM

Seeds scraped from 1 vanilla pod

Icing sugar, to taste

300ml whipping cream

150g fresh raspberry purée (sieved)

Follow directions for the shortcrust pastry.

Preheat the oven to180°C.

To make the filling, beat the butter and sugar in a bowl until light and fluffy. Add in the beaten eggs and yolk, then gently fold in the sifted flour and ground almond.

Spoon the jam into the pastry case and gently spread. Cover the jam with the sponge filling, taking care not to let the jam come up through the filling. Sprinkle blueberries and flaked almonds across the top.

Place in the middle of the oven and bake for 45-55 minutes or until the sponge is firm.

To make the Chantilly cream, mix the vanilla seeds, icing sugar and cream and whisk to soft peaks. Add the raspberry purée, and fold in without stirring completely.

Serve the pie warm with the cream.

I came up with the idea for this recipe after tasting an authentic Belgian waffle using speculoos bread dough at the Wafels and Dinges stand in Central Park, New York. Speculoos are thin, crunchy, spiced shortbread biscuits, traditionally baked in Belgium and Holland for the feast of St Nicholas, before Christmas. They make an ideal base for this easy-to-make New York dessert, although ginger biscuits or digestives also work well. The key to the filling is fresh vanilla and sweet honey mixed with rich, full-fat cream cheese. There are no eggs in the mix and there's no need to bake: just refrigerate it for a couple of hours. It will keep in the fridge for a day or two.

honey cheesecake

SERVES 6-8

200g Belgium speculoos biscuits (or ginger biscuits)

FOR THE FILLING

400g full fat cream cheese

200ml full fat crème fraiche

400ml double cream

2 vanilla pods, cut in half with seeds removed

75g honey

FOR THE TOPPING

500g mixed berries

1 tbsp icing sugar

Put the biscuits into a food processor and blitz, until they become crumbs. Spread them into the base of a non-stick, loose-bottom tin (20-22cm x 6cm), and press them down.

In a bowl, whisk together the ingredients for the cheesecake filling until thick and creamy and pour over the base. Allow to chill for 1 hour.

Remove from the tin and place the berries on top, then sprinkle with icing sugar.

End your meal with a dessert that is a real looker. I have to thank my chef friend Matt Reuther for giving me the idea for this recipe. My recipe is a little less sophisticated than his Bavarois. I use good old Nutella spread as a rich chocolate base for coffee-flavoured custard topping. Serve it in espresso cups for a creamy dessert shot. Homemade shortbread is easy to make and gives it that special finish.

coffee cups

SERVES 4

4 tbsp Nutella

FOR THE CUSTARD

3 egg yolks

75g caster sugar

20g flour

2 tbsp strong instant coffee granules

250ml milk

FOR THE SHORTBREAD BISCUITS

120g butter

60g sugar

180g plain flour

TO FINISH

300ml whipping cream

Toasted hazelnuts, chopped

Place a tablespoon of Nutella in the bottom of 4 espresso cups and place in the fridge.

For the custard, put the egg yolks and one third of the sugar in a bowl and whisk until they are pale and form a light ribbon. Sift in the flour and mix well.

In a mug, place the instant coffee granules and add just enough boiling water to be able to dissolve the granules. Combine the milk, the remaining sugar, and the coffee in a saucepan and bring to the boil.

As soon as the mixture starts to bubble, pour about one third on to the egg mixture, stirring all the time. Pour the mixture back into the pan and cook over a gentle heat, stirring continually for 2 minutes. Pour into a bowl and allow to cool.

While the custard is cooling, place the shortbread ingredients into a food processor and pulse until the mixture comes together, wrap in clingfilm and rest in the fridge for 10-15 minutes.

Preheat the oven to 180°C.

On a floured surface, roll out the shortbread dough and cut into discs approximately 4cm round. Bake for 8-10 minutes until the edge of the disc is starting to colour. Remove from the oven and dust with caster sugar.

When the custard is cooled, place into a Savoy piping bag and pipe into the espresso cups, leaving a 2cm lip on the cup. (Carefully spoon the mixture into the cups if you don't have a piping bag to hand.)

Whip 300ml whipping cream to soft peaks and spoon or pipe on to the top of the custard. Chill.

To serve, put the cups on a saucer, garnish with chopped toasted hazelnuts and place shortbread biscuits on the side.

This is a colourful pie, based on the American favourite, lemon meringue. I've replaced lemon with a bright pink rhubarb curd using beetroot juice to enhance the rhubarb's natural colour.

rhubarb meringue pie

SERVES 8-10

**FOR THE SWEET
SHORTCRUST PASTRY**

See page 16

FOR THE RHUBARB CURD

400g rhubarb

250ml beetroot juice

3 tbsp cornflour

150g caster sugar

120g butter diced

1 large free range egg

5 egg yolks

FOR THE MERINGUE

300g caster sugar

1 heaped teaspoon corn flour

5 egg whites

Follow the directions for the short sweetcrust pastry.

Preheat the oven to 180°C.

To make the filling, chop the rhubarb into 2cm pieces and place in a saucepan. Cover with beetroot juice (this helps the rhubarb keep its rich colour), bring to the boil, skim and then cook on a medium heat for 15 minutes until soft and beginning to fall apart. Strain through a sieve and push the pulp through.

Return to a clean saucepan and reduce till you have 500ml of juice.

In a bowl, mix together the cornflour and the sugar ensuring there are no lumps. Add to the rhubarb reduction and cook on a medium heat sitrring continuously, until the mixture bubbles and thickens. Remove from the heat beat in the butter. Set to one side.

Separate 5 eggs, keeping the whites to one side for the meringue. Add 1 egg and 5 yolks to the rhubarb mixture in the saucepan and beat until mixed. Return the pan to a medium heat for 4-5 minutes, and stir until the mixture thickens and starts to bubble. Remove from the heat.

Now make the meringue. In a clean bowl, whisk the egg whites to soft peaks, then add the sugar 1 tablespoon at a time. Next add the cornflour to give a lovely glossy shine to the mixture.

Fill the pastry case with the rhubarb curd and level with a spatula or spoon. Then add the meringue, starting from the sides and working inwards. Pile it high and give it a swirl, then put the pie in the oven for 20 minutes until crisp and slightly browned. Be careful not to burn the top.

Leave to rest for about 2 hours before serving.

I urge you to try this easy ice cream recipe. Just mix the ingredients together and pop it in the freezer without the fuss of having to take it out of the freezer repeatedly and stir it. Making honeycomb is simple, but take care as boiling sugar reaches a very high temperature.

apple shortbread pie & easy ice cream

SERVES 8

FOR THE SHORTBREAD PASTRY

200g butter

200g caster sugar

1 egg, plus 1 yolk

325g self-raising flour

Milk and caster sugar for brushing the pastry

FOR THE FILLING

50g butter

1 kg Bramley apples, peeled and cut into big chunks

50g dark brown sugar

Juice of 1 lemon

FOR THE HONEYCOMB

100ml water

400g sugar

2 tbsp liquid glucose

1½ tsp bicarbonate of soda

FOR THE EASY ICE CREAM

1 vanilla pod

400ml double cream

400g can skimmed condensed milk

2 tbsp honey

To make the shortbread pastry, cream the butter and sugar in a bowl until white and fluffy. Add the beaten egg and yolk, then fold in the sifted flour. Knead for a minute until smooth. Wrap the dough in cling film and chill for 1 hour.

Preheat the oven to 180°C.

For the filling, melt the butter in a medium saucepan, then add the apples, sugar and lemon juice. Cook for 10 minutes, then cool.

Grease a 20cm wide x 10cm deep round pie dish. Take two thirds of the pastry and using your fingertips press into the pie base and sides until roughly ½cm thick. Spoon the apple mixture into the tin. Roll out the remaining pastry to the size of the tin, lay on top, then crimp the edges to seal. Brush with milk and sprinkle with a handful of caster sugar.

Bake for 45 minutes. Leave to stand for 10-15 minutes before serving.

To make the honeycomb, boil the water, sugar and glucose to 160°C then add bicarbonate of soda. Pour onto a lined baking tray and allow to set.

For the ice cream, slice the vanilla pod lengthways and scrape out the black seeds. In a bowl, whisk the cream and vanilla until soft peaks form. Add the condensed milk and whisk again until combined. Break the honeycomb into large chunks and gently fold into the ice cream mix with the honey. Tip into a suitable container and freeze.

Serve the ice cream alongside a slice of pie.

Love it or hate it, rhubarb and custard are a classic British dessert combination. Under a fancy fruit topping lies my favourite creamy custard tart. The rhubarb slices are baked in the oven until they soften. I prefer rhubarb to be quite tart to balance the sweetness of the custard, but you may wish to sprinkle a little more sugar over it when baking it.

rhubarb and custard tart

SERVES 8-10

FOR THE SWEET SHORTCRUST PASTRY

See page 16

FOR THE FILLING

600ml single cream

2 vanilla pods

10 free range egg yolks

200g caster sugar

1 kg rhubarb, washed

Handful caster sugar

Follow the directions for the sweet shortcrust pastry.

Preheat the oven to 140°C.

For the filling, pour the cream into a saucepan. Split the vanilla pods and place them in the cream. Bring the cream to the boil. Take off the heat and allow to cool.

Whisk together the yolks and sugar then add the cream and mix well. Pass the mixture through a sieve into a jug.

Fill the pastry case with the custard. Carefully place in the middle of the oven and bake for 40-50 minutes, or until the custard appears set. Remove from the oven and allow to cool. Refrigerate.

Turn the oven up to 180°C.

Cut the rhubarb into neat 2.5cm slices and place on a baking tray lined with greaseproof paper. Sprinkle with a handful of caster sugar or more if you want sweeter rhubarb. I prefer tart rhubarb to complement the sweetness of the custard.

Cover the rhubarb with foil and bake for around 10-12 minutes or until it starts to go soft. Do not allow it to caramelise or start to fall apart. Remove from oven and cool.

Carefully place the rhubarb pieces onto the tart starting from the outside edge and working towards the middle in a mosaic-style pattern. Return the tart to the fridge to chill.

Serve in slices by itself or with fresh strawberries.

This twist on the classic lemon tart is a great way to finish off a meal. I've used zingy lime custard filling, paired with plump and juicy seasonal summer blackberries for decoration on top. Serve with cream or ice cream.

lime and blackberry tart

SERVES 8-10

FOR THE SWEET SHORTCRUST PASTRY

See Page 16

FOR THE LIME CUSTARD

4 medium eggs

200g caster sugar

200ml double cream

Zest and juice of 6 limes (100ml)

500g fresh blackberries

Follow directions for the sweet shortcrust pastry.

Preheat the oven to 110°C.

Now make the lime custard filling. Whisk together the egg, sugar and double cream and pass through a sieve, then add the zest and lime juice and lightly whisk again.

Pour into the pastry case and bake for 40-50 minutes or until the custard wobbles when lightly shaken.

Cool, then decorate with fresh blackberries before serving.

This recipe has been a family favourite for decades, particularly at dinner parties in the seventies. The ingredients are items you should have in the store cupboard, or be able to get without too much difficulty. Butter the bowl so the pineapple and glacé cherries don't stick when you turn it out, and the syrup in the bottom oozes over the cake. Serve with thick clotted cream.

upside down pineapple sponge pudding

SERVES 6-8

4-6 tbsp golden syrup

8-10 slices tinned pineapple rings

8-10 glace cherries

FOR THE SPONGE

200g butter

200g caster sugar

4 eggs, lightly beaten

200g self-raising flour

TO SERVE

Clotted cream

Preheat the oven to 180°C.

Pour the golden syrup into a lightly buttered round ovenproof bowl (22cm x 7cm). Arrange the pineapple by placing one in the centre then working the rest up the sides of the bowl, putting a glace cherry in the centre of each pineapple ring.

For the sponge, cream the butter and sugar, then slowly beat in the eggs one at a time, then gently fold in the flour, ensuring the mixture remains soft and light.

Carefully spread the mixture over the fruit in the bowl.

Bake in the preheated oven for 50 minutes or until a skewer inserted in the centre comes out clean. Rest for 10 minutes.

Place a large plate over the top of the bowl and turn upside down. Lift the bowl away.

Serve with clotted cream.

variation: upside down satsuma pudding

Replace the pineapple rings and glace cherries with 4 finely sliced satsumas.

Lay the satsuma slices in a saucepan and pour 4 tablespoons of water over them. Boil gently for 3 minutes, then place them on a tray using a slotted spoon. Allow to cool.

Lay the satsuma slices neatly across the base of the bowl. Pour over the golden syrup.

Follow recipe directions for the sponge, adding the juice and zest of 1 orange when you beat the eggs into the mixture.

I was inspired to make this pudding after meeting Tony Stoats at the Edinburgh Festival, where he was selling ready-to-eat organic Scottish porridge. Crumbles are a nostalgic British pud which came out of wartime rationing, when flour and sugar was scarce so breadcrumbs were used instead. The key to a good crumble is the topping and in this version the rolled Scottish porridge oats are healthy and add crunch and sweetness.

apple and raspberry crumble

SERVES 6

FOR THE FILLING

400g cooking apples, peeled, cored, quartered and cut into chunks

50g sugar

1 vanilla pod, split

Handful of raspberries

FOR THE TOPPING

125g wholemeal flour

90g rolled oats

90g butter

50g golden caster sugar

Preheat the oven to 190°C.

For the filling, put the apples into a pan with the sugar, split vanilla pod and 1 tablespoon water. Cook over a low heat for 5 minutes then place in a small ovenproof dish. Scatter the raspberries over the top of the apple. This means they will stay whole during cooking and add a nice burst of flavour.

Make the topping. Place the flour and oats in a bowl and mix well. Cut the margarine or butter into small cubes and add this to the oats and flour. Mix with your fingertips until it resembles an even crumb texture. Add the sugar and mix through.

Cover the fruit with the crumble mixture. Bake for approximately 20 minutes until the crumble is golden and apple hot.

Serve with ice cream.

Should the classic American chocolate brownie be cakey or fudgy? According to my friend Petra Barran, the fount of knowledge on all things chocolate, it should be 'almost meringue-like on top, taking in rich moist cake then plunging into a dense highly-charged fudge centre'. Her brilliant brownie recipe is the filling for this deep, rich and indulgent pie.

chocolate brownie pie

SERVES 8-10

FOR THE SHORTCRUST PASTRY

See page 14

FOR THE BROWNIE FILLING

365g dark chocolate (70% cocoa solids)

120g butter, cubed

1 tsp espresso powder

1 tsp cocoa powder

60g lightly crushed hazelnuts

625g granulated sugar

6 large eggs

100g self-raising flour

Follow directions for the shortcrust pastry.

Preheat the oven to 160°C.

Make the brownie filling. Put the chocolate and butter in a bowl sitting in a saucepan of simmering water (bain marie) and when It's almost melted, add the espresso powder and cocoa powder and stir until smooth.

Lightly toast the hazelnuts in a dry frying pan for a couple of minutes, then add to the mixture.

In a separate bowl, mix the sugar and eggs then add to the chocolate mixture. Sift in the flour and mix thoroughly. Pour into the tart case and bake for 40-45 minutes. so it's not too firm but not too liquid.

Allow to cool before serving. Serve with a dollop of crème fraiche.

In Britain, we're a bit reserved about including vegetables in sweet dishes, but this pie has been an American classic for hundreds of years. Fresh ginger, cinnamon and nutmeg enhance the pumpkin's natural sweetness. Serve with whipped cream or ice cream.

pumpkin pie

SERVES 8-10

**FOR THE SWEET
SHORTCRUST PASTRY**

See page 16

FOR THE PUMPKIN FILLING

700g mashed, cooked pumpkin passed through a sieve

200ml evaporated milk

200ml double cream

3 free-range eggs, beaten

2 egg yolks

200g dark brown sugar

½ tsp salt

½ tsp ground ginger

½ tsp ground cinnamon

½ tsp nutmeg, freshly grated

Follow directions for sweet shortcrust pastry.

Preheat oven to 160°C.

To make the filling, combine the cream, sugar and spices in a saucepan and bring to the boil then quickly whisk in the beaten eggs and egg yolks. Add the cooked pumpkin and gently stir until the ingredients are mixed.

Fill the pastry case with the pumpkin mix. Carefully place in the middle of the oven and bake for 40-45 minutes or until the mix appears set but not too firm. Remove from the oven and cover the surface liberally with grated nutmeg.

Allow to cool to room temperature before serving with a dollop of fresh cream or crème fraiche.

salted peanut caramel brownies

MAKES 9-12 SLICES

200g dark chocolate (70% cocoa solids), melted

275g light brown sugar

3 eggs

100g self-raising flour

200g dulce de leche (cooked condensed milk/caramel toffee)

100g salted peanuts, chopped

Preheat the oven to 180°C.

Melt the chocolate in a bowl sitting in a saucepan of simmering water (bain marie). Remove from the heat.

Whisk together the sugar and eggs, add the melted chocolate, and then fold in the flour.

Pour into a greased lined 20cmx20cm baking tray. Swirl the dulce de leche on top, sprinkle with peanuts and bake for 25-30 minutes.

Cool in the tray, then slice.

variation:

Why not try making a fruit and nut brownie? Replace the Dulce de Leche and salted peanuts with 150g chopped mixed nuts (hazelnuts, almonds, pistachios) and 100g dried cranberries, raisins, apricots or other dried fruit. Stir these in before pouring the mixture into the baking tray.

bread and butter pudding with banana, walnuts and chocolate

SERVES 8

220ml milk

625ml double cream

2 vanilla pods or a few drops of vanilla essence

8 egg yolks

200g caster sugar

10 thick slices of white bread, crusts cut off

55g unsalted butter, softened, plus extra for greasing

2 bananas roughly diced into 2cm chunks

30g toasted walnuts, roughly chopped

55g dark chocolate chips

Icing sugar for dusting

Pour the milk and cream into a saucepan. Split the vanilla pods and place them in the saucepan. If using vanilla essence add this to the milk and cream. Bring to the boil, take off the heat and allow to cool.

In a bowl, whisk the egg yolks and sugar, then using a sieve, strain the cream, milk and vanilla pods into the eggs and sugar, stirring continuously.

Butter the slices of bread and cut each piece into four triangles.

Grease a baking dish (28cm x 18m x 4cm). Layer the triangles of bread, buttered-side up, on the base of the dish and ensure they overlap. Sprinkle with banana, walnuts and chocolate chips. Repeat this process until all the bread, bananas, walnuts and chocolate chips are used up.

Carefully pour over the custard, then leave to stand for 20 minutes, pushing the bread into the liquid occasionally so the bread can soak up the custard.

While the pudding is soaking, preheat the oven to 175°C.

Place the baking dish in a larger baking tray half-filled with boiling water and place in the oven for 30 minutes until cooked but with a slight wobble. The triangle tips of bread poking out of the pudding will crisp up nicely during baking.

Do not allow the custard to overcook otherwise it will scramble. Let the pudding rest for 10 minutes once it is removed from the oven.

Dust with icing sugar before serving.

When I worked at the Light Bar in Shoreditch, London, Caipirinha cocktail was my favourite drink. Here, I've combined the boozy cocktail flavour of Brazilian sugar cane rum and limes with a popular dessert from the Florida Keys in America. I've used regular limes instead of the smaller, paler and sharper Key variety. The crunchy granola and chocolate digestive base is good enough to eat on its own, but combined with the creamy filling gives a real tropical flavour.

key lime pie with caipirinha sorbet

SERVES 8

FOR THE CRUST

10 dark chocolate digestive biscuits

100g granola

125g butter, melted

FOR THE FILLING

4 egg yolks

300ml condensed milk

200g full-fat cream cheese

200g ricotta

Juice and zest of 4 limes

FOR THE SORBET

100ml water

100g caster sugar

3 limes, juiced

50ml Cachaca liquor (made from fermented sugar cane juice)

Preheat the oven to 180°C.

In a food processor, blend the biscuits and granola and melted butter and mix well. Press the mixture into the bottom of a greased, high sided springform pie tin (20-22cm x 5-7cm). Bake for 5 minutes. You can also crush the biscuits and granola by putting them in a sealed plastic bag and sqashing with a rolling pin.

For the filling, whisk the egg yolks then gradually add the condensed milk, ricotta and cream cheese until smooth. Add the lime juice, then pour the mixture into the tin.

Bake in the oven for 20 minutes, then allow to cool. Sprinkle with lime zest then refrigerate for 4 hours.

For the sorbet, heat the water and sugar together in a saucepan until the sugar dissolves. Add the lime juice and Cachaca and mix. Churn in an ice cream machine or pour the mixture into a large plastic bowl and freeze, mixing every 10 minutes with a wooden spoon to break up the ice crystals.

Serve the pie in thick wedges with a scoop of the sorbet.

dips and dressings

As a lover of 'a little bit on the side' with all my pies, I think sauces and dips add another dimension to a dish, complementing and enhancing the flavours. Every country in the world has its signature accompaniments, from the spicy sour cream-based Ranch dressings popular in the USA, to the Middle Eastern favourite hummus, now commonplace in Britain.

It's easy to reach for a bottle of sauce, but I promise it's much more satisfying to make it yourself, then you can be sure to strike gold in the flavour and freshness department.

I make no apologies that some of the sauces in this chapter are very British. Salad Cream, Piccalilli, Tomato Ketchup and Brown Sauce have all had a strong heritage on British dining tables for the past century.

Go into any home in Britain and you'll probably find a bottle of brown sauce (or HP sauce, its most popular brand name) in the cupboard. Some say its sweet, tangy, vinegary flavour is an acquired taste. But once you've made my brown sauce, you'll never go back to the bottle.

I've also looked to other countries for inspiration with my dips, including the cheesy French favourite Fromage Fort, and my quick and easy Hummus.

This barbecue recipe has its roots in South Africa. The aubergines, or eggplants, are delicious cooked on the barbecue, while the toasted cumin brings out the flavour, especially when served with warm, Roosterkoek dough balls grilled fresh over the barbecue. If you're unsure about making your own bread any flatbread will work.

spicy aubergine dip with roosterkoek bread

SERVES 10-12

FOR THE DIP

2 aubergines

2 tsp cumin

1-2 garlic cloves, chopped

400ml Greek yoghurt

Juice and zest of half a lemon

Salt and coarsely ground black pepper to taste

FOR THE ROOSTERKOEK BREAD

400g plain flour, plus extra for dusting

1 x 5g pack dried yeast

1 tsp salt

2 tsp caster sugar

50ml vegetable oil

Olive oil, for brushing

Place aubergines on the barbecue (or oven preheated to 180°C). Cook for 30-40 minutes, turning from time to time. Cut in half and allow to cool.

Meanwhile, place cumin in a dry pan and toast on the stove for 5 minutes.

Chop the cooked aubergines and mash them together with the garlic, toasted cumin, Greek yoghurt, lemon zest and juice. Add salt and pepper to taste. Set to one side.

To make the bread, mix the yeast, sugar and 100ml warm water and stir. The mixture will start to foam after 5 minutes or so. In a separate bowl, mix together the flour and salt then add the oil and the yeast mix. Add enough warm water to make a slightly moist dough. Turn the dough out on a floured surface and knead for about 5 minutes. Place the dough in an oiled bowl and cover with cling film or a damp cloth. Leave to rise for about 1 hour.

Divide the mixture into roughly 12 equal pieces and shape into slightly flattened balls. Place on to a floured board or lightly greased tray and cover again with a damp cloth or clingfilm and leave to rise for a further 15 minutes.

Gently lift the dough balls and place on the preheated barbecue (or a griddle), turning a couple of times until the bread is nicely marked and well puffed up and becomes crusty on the outside.

Brush with a little olive oil and serve straight away alongside the dip.

Depending on what part of the world you're from, brown sauce will mean something different to you. In France it's more of a meat-stock based sauce. In Scandinavia, it's a gravy poured over meatballs. Americans have a similar steak sauce and Canadians use it on meat. But this recipe is based on the classic British bottled brown sauce, better-known by its popular Heinz brand name HP sauce. For more than 100 years we've been serving it with everything from bacon and eggs at breakfast to cheese on toast. The vinegar gives the sauce its tanginess and the treacle and sugar add the sweetness. Personally, I love a dollop of my fresh brown sauce with a pork pie or pasty.

brown sauce

MAKES 2 X 500G JARS

1 tbsp vegetable oil

2 banana shallots, roughly chopped

2 tomatoes, roughly chopped

50g dates, stoned

2 Bramley apples peeled, cored, quartered and roughly chopped

3 tbsp tamarind pulp

A thumb-size piece of freshly-grated root ginger

1 star anise

4 whole cloves

4 black peppercorns

1 bay leaf

A pinch of cayenne pepper

1 tbsp mustard powder

2 tbsp flour

2 tbsp Muscovado sugar

2 tbsp black treacle

700ml malt vinegar

Salt and pepper

In a saucepan over a medium heat, heat the oil and then sweat off the shallots for 5 minutes without colour. Then add the tomatoes, dates, apples, 200ml water, tamarind pulp, ginger and the next six ingredients. Bring to the boil and simmer gently for 10-15 minutes until everything cooks and mixes together.

Pass the mix through a fine sieve, extracting as much liquid and goodness as possible. Discard the pulp.

Return the liquid to a clean pan and bring to the boil. Stir in the flour, bring to the boil and add the sugar, treacle and vinegar. Cook for around 15 minutes, stirring every now and then until thickened.

Season to taste.

Once cooled, store in sterilised jars for up to 3 weeks.

For mayonnaise snobs, salad cream is its poor relation. But I love it. Created in Britain in the 1920s when rationing meant eggs were scarce or expensive, the salad cream uses the whole egg rather than just the yolk. In this recipe, I've added whipping cream for extra thick texture. Keep in a sterilised jar in the fridge and it will stay fresh for two or three days.

salad cream

MAKES 1X 500G JAR

2 tsp English mustard

4 tsp sugar

A pinch of salt

A pinch of white pepper

1 tsp flour

2 eggs

100ml cider vinegar

150ml whipping cream

Lemon juice to taste

Sprinkle of cayenne pepper
(to garnish)

Place a Pyrex bowl over a saucepan of simmering water. Whisk together the mustard, sugar, salt, pepper, flour, eggs and vinegar.

Whisk continuously until thickened and glossy but do not overcook the eggs. Allow to cool, then whisk in the cream and lemon juice.

Store in a sterilised jar in the fridge until needed.

Wherever you travel in the world you'll find a bottle of Heinz tomato ketchup. So why make your own when it's so easy to reach for the bottle? Well, I reckon it's more of a treat to offer your friends and family a home-made variety and my version is bursting with tomato tang. Don't scrimp on the tomatoes, use the best quality you can afford. It makes all the difference to the taste.

tomato ketchup

MAKES 1 X 400ML JAR

2 tbsp olive oil

1 banana shallot, finely diced

3 cloves of crushed garlic

400g chopped tinned tomatoes

1 tbsp Worcestershire sauce

2 tbsp maple syrup

Heat some olive oil in a pan. Sweat off the shallot, then add the garlic, followed by the tinned tomatoes, Worcestershire sauce and maple syrup.

Break up the tomatoes and allow the mixture to reduce and thicken for 30-40 minutes. Set to one side.

Serve along with my burger (page 50) or home-made fries. Store in a sterilised jar in the fridge.

In Britain, we've been making and eating our own western version of Indian pickle since the 18th century, when it was called 'Paco-Lilla' or 'India Pickle'. Americans make similar relishes using peppers, gherkins or green tomatoes as popular toppings for burgers and hot dogs. For this version, I've used the traditional ingredients of cauliflower and onions for the crunch and mustard and turmeric for the spice. Stored in a sterilised jar in the fridge, this Piccalilli will keep fresh for several months.

piccalilli

MAKES 2 X 700G JARS

1 cauliflower, broken into small florets

30 silverskin onions

395g runner beans, diced

1 cucumber, peeled, de-seeded and diced

2 medium carrots, diced

200g salt

415ml cider vinegar

207ml malt vinegar

340g caster sugar

56g English mustard

28g turmeric

3 tbsp grain mustard

4 tbsp cornflour

Put the vegetables in a bowl and cover with the salt and 1.4 litres water. Leave for 2 hours (this brining process will help the vegetables to stay crispy for longer).

Drain, rinse and dry the vegetables. Keep to one side.

Combine the remaining ingredients, except the cornflour, in a large saucepan and bring to the boil.

Whisk the cornflour with 4 tablespoons of cold water, until you have a thin paste. Pour this into the spice mix and whisk rapidly, until the sauce has thickened.

Add the vegetables and cook for 5 minutes over a medium heat.

Pour into sterilised jars and refrigerate. This Piccalilli will keep for several months.

A popular Middle Eastern dish served as a starter with pita bread. I've substituted the traditional ingredients of sesame seed paste (tahini) and chick peas, with ground almonds and breadcrumbs, to create an easy dip which works well with flatbreads and crudités, but can also be served as a side dressing for barbecued lamb.

almond hummus

SERVES 8-10

2 slices white bread

1 tbsp minced garlic

250g ground almonds

Juice of 3 lemons

600ml olive oil

Soak the bread in water for a minute.

In a blender or food processor, blitz the garlic, almonds and bread together. Add lemon juice to taste and adjust consistency with water if necessary.

When smooth, very slowly add olive oil as if you were making mayonnaise.

Serve with flatbread, crudités or pita. Also works very well served alongside BBQ lamb.

In our house, there's always loads of cheese left over after Christmas, and this garlicky cheese spread, served with toast, is a tasty way to use it up. Meaning 'strong cheese' in French, the riper the cheese used, the better the flavour. Popular cheeses to include are Brie, Camembert, Parmigiano-Reggiano, Swiss cheese, and even goat's cheese. Be careful if you're using blue cheese as too much can drown the flavours of the wine and garlic.

fromage fort

SERVES 6-8

2 cloves garlic, crushed

700g leftover cheese (the stronger the better), chopped

150ml white wine

2 tbsp softened butter

Black pepper

Blend the garlic in a food processor then add all other ingredients until creamy.

Serve with toast.

This gets better with age and is delicious melted on toast as well!

inspired creations

In this chapter, I have endeavoured to put my own stamp on some regional and international classics.

My culinary journeys around Britain have exposed me to exciting flavour combinations and dishes. And during my gastronomic road trip across America, I was constantly amazed by the variety of food on offer as I travelled from state to state: the Deep South with its spicy jambalaya; the west coast of California with its Mexican influences; the Cuban flavours of Florida.

The emphasis of these recipes is still all about sharing. Some of the dishes like my Confit Duck Leg or Dauphinoise take time to prepare, but they are so worth it.

Created by my friend Nichola Smith who runs Healthy Yummies catering company in London, this dish uses scallops freshly caught from West Bay, Dorset and vegetables foraged from the sea shore. Samphire is a marsh grass with a salty flavour and is available in most supermarkets. You may have difficulty sourcing its leafier cousins purslane and sea aster unless you know a seashore forager, but you can replace them with more samphire. The sea vegetables bring a salty crunch to the flavour of bacon and scallops, while the celeriac adds a comforting creaminess.

dived scallops, celeriac puree, bacon and seashore vegetables

SERVES 4 (FOR A STARTER)

FOR THE CELERIAC PUREE

1 medium celeriac, peeled and cut into 2.5cm cubes

620ml whole milk

210ml double cream

2 bay leaves

1 sprig of fresh thyme

¼tsp freshly grated nutmeg

Salt and pepper, to taste

FOR THE SCALLOPS AND VEGETABLES

8 large scallops

2 rashers of smoked streaky bacon, preferably Gloucester Old Spot

40g butter

1 lemon

150g seashore vegetables (sea beet, sea purslane, stone crop and samphire)

1 tbsp mild olive oil

8 scallop shells, well cleaned

Put the celeriac, milk, cream, bay leaves, thyme and nutmeg in a pan and cook on a medium heat with the lid on, until the celeriac is soft. Remove from the heat, remove the herbs and blend the celeriac with a little of the liquor in the batches until all of the celeriac is used up. You should have a puree consistency. Add salt and pepper to taste and set aside.

Wash the scallops and place between two pieces of kitchen paper to absorb excess water. Place one rasher of bacon on top of the other and finely dice. Add to a hot frying pan without oil and toss for a minute or so until just cooked. Remove and place on some kitchen towel and set aside.

Cut the butter into cubes, cut the lemon in half and set aside. Sort through the seashore vegetables and pick out any woody stalk and set aside. Put the puree in a pan and gently heat through. Season both side of the scallops.

Put a large frying pan on a medium heat, until just before smoking, add the oil and scallops. Whilst the scallops are on, place 1 dessertspoon of the celeriac puree into each shell. Once the underside of the scallops have browned, turn them over and add the bacon.

After 30 seconds, add the butter and lemon juice. When the butter has melted, add the seashore vegetables and toss. Turn the heat off.

Place one scallop on top of the celeriac puree; add a spoon of the brown butter with bacon and the seashore vegetables. Repeat for other scallops.

A traditional dish from Louisiana in the Deep South of the USA, jambalaya is a mix of vegetables, meat and rice similar to the Spanish paella. Like the dish itself, the name is a mouthful and there are many theories about where it came from. My favourite is the old wives' tale about a gentleman travelling through New Orleans who stopped at an inn just as they were running out of food and asked the cook, who was called Jean Balayez, to rustle something up. The resulting dish became known as 'Jean Balayez.' I was taught how to cook it by brothers Eric and Paul Theard, who sell traditional Louisiana home cooking from their Foodie Call truck in the streets of New Orleans. It's a really filling dish, offering a different flavour in every mouthful with the juices from the chicken and prawns mixing with the spices and tomatoes and soaking into the rice.

andy's jambalaya

SERVES 6

FOR THE JAMBALAYA

6 chicken thigh joints, bone in, skin on

200g Andouille sausage, sliced or chorizo

2-3 tbsp olive oil

1 large onion, peeled and cut into slices and roughly chopped the same size as the peppers

1 red pepper, sliced

1 yellow pepper, sliced

1 green pepper, sliced

1 stick of celery, sliced

4 large garlic cloves, peeled and sliced

½ tsp smoked paprika

½ tsp cayenne pepper

50g sun-dried tomatoes

1 tbsp tomato purée

225g brown basmati rice, washed

500ml chicken stock

Salt and pepper

200g raw tiger prawns

FOR THE GARNISH

3 chopped spring onions

2 tbsp chopped parsley

2 tbsp chopped tarragon

Preheat oven to 170°C.

Season the chicken thighs and seal them off in a casserole dish, making sure the skin is golden-brown. Transfer them to a warm plate then seal off the Andouille sausage (or chorizo) until browned a little, then transfer to the plate with the chicken.

Heat the olive oil in the casserole then add the onions, peppers, celery and garlic to the pan and sweat off until softened. Add the spices, sun-dried tomatoes and tomato purée and cook for a further 5 minutes. Pour over the rice and mix thoroughly, making sure all the rice is coated in oil and juices.

Add the stock, season and bring to the boil. Add the chicken and sausage.

Cover and bake for 55 minutes. Remove from the oven, add the prawns, cover and return for 5 minutes. Leave to rest for 10 minutes.

Remove the lid and garnish with spring onions, parsley and tarragon. Serve immediately.

smoke-roasted sea trout with horseradish potatoes and beetroot dressing

The components of this dish and the dressing blend well – the intense flavour of toasted pine nuts, peppery tarragon, the heat of fresh horseradish and sweet maple syrup. Take care when adding fresh horseradish to the mix as it has an intense flavour and you don't want to overdo it, so add a bit at a time and taste it as you go along. The smoked trout is already cooked, so simply fry it off on both sides to give it a crisp golden finish. If you have trouble buying smoked trout, smoked salmon or smoked mackerel also work.

SERVES 4

400g new potatoes

4 x smoke-roasted sea trout fillets

1 tbsp olive oil

1 tbsp natural Greek yoghurt

Juice of 1 lemon

2 tbsp chives, finely chopped

1 tbsp fresh horseradish or 2 tbsp creamed horseradish

Salt and pepper

FOR THE DRESSING

50g toasted pine nuts

150g beetroot, cooked, finely chopped

1 banana shallot, finely chopped

1 tbsp chopped tarragon

3 tbsp olive oil

1 tbsp maple syrup

1 tbsp balsamic vinegar

Salt and pepper

Boil the potatoes until cooked, drain and allow to cool a little.

In a frying pan, heat the olive oil, then fry the trout fillet for 2-3 minutes on both sides. Remove from the pan and keep warm until needed.

In a bowl, mix the yoghurt, lemon and chives. Season and add horseradish to your liking and mix. Set to one side.

To make the dressing, toast the pine nuts, then combine in a bowl with the beetroot, shallots and tarragon. Make a sweet dressing with oil, maple syrup and balsamic vinegar and season to taste. Toss together.

Quarter the potatoes and mix them with the yoghurt mixture.

To serve, make a small bed of potato on a plate. Place the fillet on top and spoon the beetroot dressing around.

In my opinion, seaweed is an underrated vegetable of the sea which deserves to be used more in home cooking. I was taught this recipe by Welsh seashore forager Jonathan Williams who runs Cafe Môr in west Wales. He has the best job in the world, combing the beautiful beaches of Pembrokeshire for tasty Welsh seaweed to use in his flatbreads. Bladderwrack is the most common and recognisable seaweed on our shores, but make sure you wash it thoroughly to get rid of all the sand. If you can't get bladderwrack, use any seaweed. I use it as a bed to help steam the fresh sea bream. The dulse seaweed adds a peppery taste to the dish. If you're thinking of foraging for your own seaweed, check it's an edible variety before cooking it.

sea bream steamed on a bed of bladderwrack with lemon

SERVES 2

1 medium sea bream

2-3 large handfuls bladderwrack

160ml water

2 lemons, quartered

Cherry tomatoes

1 handful of rocket samphire

FOR THE DULSE SAUCE

103g butter

5 tbsp dulse seaweed

FOR THE FLATBREADS

2 handfuls flour

Pinch of salt

Pinch cayenne pepper

4 tbsp olive oil

To cook the sea bream, place a pan on a medium to high heat.

Wash the bladderwrack (if you can't get hold of bladderwrack, any seaweed will do). Place the seaweed in the pan, along with half the water. Put the fish on top of the seaweed and place the quartered lemons around the fish.

Cover the pan with a lid, or if you don't have a lid just use tin foil. Leave this to steam for 15-20 minutes.

To make the dulse sauce, place the butter in a frying pan and allow it to begin to melt. Finely chop the dulse seaweed and add it to the butter. Continue to fry for 5 minutes.

For the flat bread, place the flour, sea salt and cayenne pepper into a bowl, along with the olive oil and mix through. Add the remaining water until it begins to form a dough. You may need to add more flour or water so the dough is the right consistency. Roll out the dough into a circle and put it onto a preheated frying pan for a couple of minutes on each side, or until it turns golden brown.

Remove the fish from the pan and place into the dulse sauce, along with 3 of the lemon wedges, squeezing the juice out of them. Spoon the dulse sauce over the fish.

Serve with chopped cherry tomatoes and rocket samphire. Use the flat bread as a wrap to put all of the ingredients in.

slow roasted lamb shoulder with feta salsa

SERVES 6

FOR THE LAMB

120ml extra virgin olive oil

1 tsp cumin

2 garlic cloves, crushed

Zest of 1 lemon

Salt and pepper

1.5kg shoulder of lamb

FOR THE SALSA

120ml olive oil

2 garlic cloves, slice as thin as possible

Zest of 1 lemon, thinly sliced

200g barrel-aged feta cheese

FOR THE VEGETABLES

1 courgette, diced into 1cm cubes

1 red onion, diced into 1cm cubes

1 red pepper, de-seeded and diced into 1cm cubes

400g tinned chickpeas

1 tbsp extra virgin olive oil

FOR THE YOGHURT SAUCE

1 mini cucumber (or 1/2 cucumber)

500ml Greek yoghurt

3 tbsp mint (fresh or dried), finely chopped

Mix together the olive oil, cumin, garlic, lemon zest and a pinch of salt and pepper then rub over the lamb. Cover in a bowl and leave to marinate overnight.

For the salsa, in a small saucepan bring the oil, garlic and lemon zest to a very gentle simmer. This will infuse the oil. Leave overnight.

The next day, preheat the oven to 220°C.

Place the lamb in an ovenproof dish and put in the oven for 35 minutes. Take out of the oven, baste, cover the tray with foil then return to the oven turning the heat down to 150°C. Cook for 2½ hours or until the meat is falling away from the bone.

While the lamb is cooking, heat some olive oil and gently sauté the vegetables until cooked and they begin to colour. Add the chickpeas, season and if a little dry, add a touch of virgin olive oil. Allow to cool and then gently reheat before serving.

Remove the lamb from oven, rest for 30 minutes still covered with foil to keep warm.

For the yoghurt sauce, dice the cucumber into ½cm cubes and add to the yoghurt along with the chopped mint.

Season and mix thoroughly. Refrigerate until needed.

To finish the salsa, reheat the oil and when it's gently simmering, remove from heat and crumble the feta cheese in and stir until mixed. Season and squeeze in the juice of 1 lemon. Keep warm.

With the lamb rested, take the meat from the bone and shred it with two forks. Pour the feta salsa over the meat.

Serve alongside the warmed vegetables and yoghurt dip.

I've taken this classic American dish upmarket by using quail instead of chicken. In Los Angeles, celebrity chef Ludo Lefebvre, who runs pop-ups and a gourmet fried chicken truck, taught me how to get the best crunch from fried chicken. The secret is to add a little buttermilk to the seasoned flour coating, which makes it lumpy. Soaking the quail overnight in buttermilk mix makes it really moist. For a really sweet peach salsa, peel the bitter skins from the fruit before dicing it.

southern fried quail with peach salsa

SERVES 4

4 quails, spatchcocked and halved

900ml buttermilk

1 tbsp dried mixed herbs

FOR THE CRISPY COATING

750g self-raising flour

Salt and pepper

½ tsp cayenne pepper

1 tsp smoked paprika

1 tbsp dried oregano

½ tsp all spice

Oil for deep-frying

FOR THE PEACH SALSA

4 ripe peaches, peeled, cored and cut into 1cm dice

1 red onion, chopped and cut into 1cm dice

Zest and juice of 1 lime

1 tsp basil

1 tsp mint

1 tsp parsley

3 tbsp extra virgin olive oil

1 tbsp cider vinegar

To marinate the quail, combine the mixed herbs and buttermilk in a large bowl, season with salt and pepper and add the quail. Cover with cling film and leave for 8 hours or overnight.

To make the crispy coating, combine all dry ingredients and 4-5 tbsp of the buttermilk marinade. Fold through gently without mixing to create clumps in the flour.

Remove the quail from the marinade, roll in the floury mixture then dip in the marinade again and then return to the flour. Use some pressure to create a firm coating.

Deep fry at 180°C for 8 minutes then allow to rest for 10 minutes.

For the salsa, mix all ingredients together and season. Serve the quail alongside the salsa.

How to spatchcock. The first step to spatchcock quail is to remove the backbone. Place the quail breast-side down and use scissors to cut along either side of the backbone and through the ribs. Once you've removed the bone, the quail can be laid flat.

My style of cooking is all about simple food you can try at home, but this dish is the closest I've come to creating something that wouldn't look out of place on a restaurant menu. The halibut, a firm-fleshed fish popular in North America, is topped with the chiltepil garnish, a dry toasted salsa mix of nuts and spices taught to me by Abraham Ortega of the legendary Antojitos Carmen Mexican restaurant in Los Angeles. The fish is served on the bed of refried, mashed pinto beans with homemade Mexican dips of spicy tomato salsa and creamy guacamole. If you can't get hold of halibut, try any other firm-fleshed fish.

halibut steak, chorizo, refried beans and guacamole

SERVES 2

2 x 150g halibut fillets

Olive oil

Knob of butter

Lemon juice

Chiltepil to garnish
(a dry salsa combining 1 tsp
seasame seeds,1 tsp peanuts,
chopped, and ½ tsp garlic
powder or chopped garlic,
toasted together in a pan)

FOR THE GUACAMOLE

2 small shallots

6 Jalapeño slices

1 large ripe avocado

1 tbsp soured cream

Juice of 1 lime

FOR THE BEANS

1 tbsp finely diced onion

50g diced chorizo

150g cooked pinto beans

100-200ml chicken or
vegetable stock

FOR THE SALSA

1 fresh ripe tomato, seeded
and diced

1 tbsp diced red onion

3 black olives, diced

Fresh coriander, chopped, to
taste

1 tbsp olive oil

1 tbsp balsamic vinegar

For the guacamole, in a food processor, blend the shallot and Jalapeño. Add the flesh of the avocado, soured cream and lime juice. Blend until very smooth. Season to taste. Store in the fridge.

For the refried beans, sweat the onion off without colour until softened. Add the chorizo and cook for 3-4 minutes. Mash the beans and then add to the onion and chorizo, continue to cook till hot. You will need to let the mixture down with chicken or vegetable stock. Season to taste and keep warm.

For the Salsa, combine the tomato (concasse), onion and olives. Add the olive oil, balsamic and coriander and gently toss.

Preheat oven to 180°C.

Next, heat the olive oil in a frying pan and place the halibut fillets skin side down and fry for 5 minutes until crispy. Then season with salt and pepper, add a knob of butter and squeeze of lemon and place in the oven for 7-8 minutes.

To assemble: on a large plate make a bed of refried beans, place 2 tablespoons of guacamole next to it and slide through with a spoon.

Place the halibut skin side up on top of the beans and drizzle the salsa lightly around the plate. Garnish the halibut with the dry salsa.

The idea of combining main ingredients from the land and sea first started in America in the 1960s, when lobster and steak dishes started appearing on menus as surf and turf. For this dish I've taken free-range chicken from the land and juicy mussels from the sea, cooking them in the same pan to get the lovely flavours of the juices mixing together. When buying mussels, check the shells are tightly closed, as this means they are alive and fresh. Once they are cooked, throw away any that do not open easily. The baby gem lettuce is a great way to catch all the sauce poured over it.

chicken and mussels in cider with baby gem lettuce

SERVES 4

4 large chicken thighs, skin on

50g butter

4 shallots, finely chopped

5 cloves of garlic, thinly sliced

3 tbsp cider vinegar

300ml dry cider

300ml chicken stock

1 bunch of fresh tarragon, stems removed and chopped

50ml crème fraiche

500g mussels, cleaned and debearded

150g asparagus tips

Salt and pepper

Juice of 1 lemon

4 Baby Gem lettuce hearts

Season the chicken thighs then seal them, skin side down, in a frying pan, for at least 8-10 minutes, making sure that you render the fat and get it nice and crispy.

Remove from the pan and put on to a tray.

In the same pan, sweat off the shallots and garlic in the butter. Add the vinegar and reduce until nearly evaporated. Add the cider and chicken stock to the pan and reduce by half. Add the chicken, half the tarragon and crème fraiche, then cover and simmer for 20-25 minutes until the chicken is tender.

Remove the lid, turn up the heat and add the mussels and asparagus. Return the lid to the pan for about 3-4 minutes until the mussels have opened. Season and add the lemon juice and remaining tarragon.

In a large bowl, lay the lettuce on the bottom, then ladle the chicken and the mussels over, followed by the asparagus. Bring the sauce to the boil and pour over the top. Serve.

Comfort food at its best, this dish uses the cheaper brisket cut of beef. This cut can be tough, but stick to my recipe and it'll melt in your mouth. The velouté sauce that the meat is cooked in is the first sauce I learnt how to make at catering college and uses a meat stock and flour paste to thicken it. Use a potato ricer on your potato and celeriac to make the creamiest mash and avoid any lumps.

boiled brisket with celeriac mash and cream sauce

SERVES 6

FOR THE MEAT

1 kg beef brisket, salted

2 carrots, peeled and sliced

1 onion, peeled and sliced

3 sticks celery, sliced

3 sprigs fresh thyme

FOR THE SAUCE

25g butter

25g plain flour

600ml cooking stock (from meat)

100ml double cream

1 tbsp capers

100g chopped gherkins

Bunch of flat-leaf parsley, chopped

Juice of 1 lemon

Pepper

FOR THE MASH

1 large celeriac, peeled and cut into equal chunks

1 large potato, peeled and cut into equal chunks

450ml milk

Salt and pepper

In a large saucepan cover the brisket with water and bring to the boil then refresh in cold water. Fill the pan with fresh water, return the brisket to the pan and add the vegetables and fresh thyme. Bring back to the boil, skimming any scum from the surface.

Simmer for 3 hours until tender then allow the brisket to rest in its stock and keep warm. Strain off 600ml of the cooking stock.

Make the sauce. In a pan cook the butter and flour to make a roux. Gradually add the stock to make a velouté. Cook out for 5 minutes then add the cream. Season with pepper. Just before serving, bring the sauce to the boil and add the capers, gherkins, parsley and lemon juice.

For the mash, add the celeriac and potatoes to a pan, cover with the milk and boil, then simmer for 20 minutes until cooked. Drain and mash, adding a little of the cooking milk. Season.

To serve, slice the brisket, place on top of the mash and spoon some of the sauce over.

I don't know many people who don't like roast pork. Lean pale pink flesh, firm white fat and smooth rind are signs of a good quality meat. Personally I love the combination of fruit and meat in this dish, and what better way to celebrate than with apple and mustard mash? Cooking the pork in cider not only infuses an apple-like tenderness, but the juices can be reduced to make a lovely gravy. I prefer to use Granny Smith apples for the sauce as they keep their shape and texture.

roasted loin of pork with apple and mustard mash

SERVES 6-8

FOR THE PORK

2kg pork loin

Salt and pepper

2 onions, peeled and roughly chopped

Large bunch of fresh sage

Olive oil

1 litre cider

FOR THE APPLE & MUSTARD MASH

750g potatoes

Milk to cover

750g Granny Smith apples, peeled, cored, quartered and each quarter cut into six chunks

100g butter

1 tbsp dark brown sugar

2 heaped tbsp wholegrain mustard

Preheat the oven to 180°C.

Season the pork and seal in a large pan. In an ovenproof dish place the onions and sage, drizzle with olive oil to coat. Place the pork on top and transfer to oven and bake for 15 minutes. Turn down the oven to 160°C, pour over the cider and bake for a further 50 minutes, basting every 10 minutes.

Rest the pork in a loosely covered dish for 30 minutes. Keep the onion sage and cider juice for gravy, reducing it if needed.

For the mash, in a saucepan cover the potatoes in milk and simmer until cooked. Drain and mash.

Fry the apple chunks in butter and sugar until gently softened, keeping their shape. Mix the apple and potato together, add the mustard and season. Slice the loin in thick slices and serve on top of the mash. Spoon juice over the pork.

This dish needs a bit of forward planning, as the duck has to chill in a fridge with the salt, garlic and herbs for 24 hours before cooking. Confit is an old French way of preserving meat in fat, so it's not a dish to be eaten every day. But if you love a deep succulent flavour to your birds it's worth the fuss. Once cooked, the duck will keep in the fridge for a month. And when you're ready to eat it, bake it in the oven. Red cabbage and Dauphinoise potatoes are a great accompaniment.

confit duck leg

SERVES 4

4 duck legs

150g-200g flaked
sea salt

2 sprigs of
rosemary

2 sprigs of thyme

A bulb of garlic,
peeled

800g goose or
duck fat

3 black
peppercorns

In a dish lay the duck legs skin side up and cover with the salt, 1 sprig each of rosemary and thyme and 2 cloves of crushed garlic. Cover with clingfilm and refrigerate for 24hrs.

The next day wash the duck legs in water to remove the salt and then pat dry.

Preheat the oven to 140°c.

In a casserole dish, heat the fat until melted, then add the duck legs making sure they are completely covered. Add the remaining herbs, the halved garlic cloves and peppercorns, then cover.

Bake gently in the oven for around 3 hours or until tender (the size of the legs can vary cooking time).

Once cooked, allow to cool slightly. Place the duck carefully into a container and then strain the fat over. Cover and store for up to 3-4 weeks in the fridge (which also helps to develop the flavour).

To reheat, take the duck legs out, scrape away any excess fat and bake for 30 minutes at 180°C until the skin is nice and crispy.

Serve with Red Cabbage and Dauphinoise potatoes.

This is one of those side dishes I've grown to love as I've got older. It's a great winter warmer that goes well with duck or pork, and is also a Christmas classic served with cold meats on Boxing Day. The beauty of this dish is that it improves with age. Make it the day before, and the cabbage will soften and absorb the flavours. Some people like to add sultanas to the apples, but I prefer pears for a fruitier flavour.

red cabbage with apples and pears

SERVES 4

500g finely shredded cabbage

2 Granny Smith apples, peeled and cut into 2cm dice

1 tbsp Muscovado sugar

200ml red wine

2 pears, peeled and cut into 2cm dice

100ml Crème de Cassis

Salt and pepper

Place all the ingredients except the pears and Crème de Cassis in a casserole dish and and bring to the boil on a medium heat. Cover and cook for 30 minutes.

Remove the lid, add the Crème de Cassis and pears and cook for a further 15 minutes or until most of the liquid, but not all, has evaporated. Season to taste and serve.

When I started my first proper restaurant job as a commis veg chef at Reeds Restaurant in Kent, I was taught how to cook this dish by my friend James McLean. Later, when I went to college, my lecturer Gary Goldsmith said it was the best Dauphinoise he had ever tasted. You can't rush a good Dauphinoise. You need to make sure every layer of potatoes is seasoned well. It takes time, but done well, it is totally worth it. I could sit down with a spoon and eat it all day.

dauphinoise potatoes

SERVES 4-6

1.5kg floury potatoes, such as Maris Piper

500ml double cream

3 cloves of garlic

Sprig of fresh thyme

Sprig of fresh rosemary

1 small onion, peeled and halved

150g Gruyere cheese

Preheat oven to 160°C.

Peel the potatoes and place whole into cold water. Pour the cream into a pan, then add the garlic, thyme and rosemary and the onion. Heat to boiling point and simmer for 5 minutes, allow to cool slightly, then strain into a jug or another pan. Slice the potato directly into the warm flavoured cream.

Once well mixed, begin to layer the potato in the dish, remembering to grate Gruyere cheese between each layer and seasoning as you go. Once the dish is full and you've used all the cheese, pour a little cream over the top to help the cooking process.

Bake in a bain marie (water bath) by placing the dish into a larger dish and filling halfway with hot water then put in the oven for 1-1.5 hours.

Once cooked, rest for 10 minutes then serve.

pork belly and creamed beans

The hero of this dish is free-range pork belly. Although it is one of the cheaper cuts of meat, I love cooking pork belly, as the higher fat content gives it a delicious taste. Slow-roasting the meat on a bed of onions provides extra flavour and also stops the pork burning on the bottom of the roasting pan. The idea for this dish came from Jamie Berger of the Pitt Cue Co who I met at London's Real Food Market selling smoky, tender pulled pork inspired by his home in Georgia, USA. Cooked this way, it is so soft and tender that it falls apart with a fork. And the creamed beans are a posh type of baked beans cooked in cream and rosemary sauce.

SERVES 6

FOR THE PORK BELLY

1.5kg pork belly, skin on, no bones, skin scored

3 tbsp olive oil

1½ tbsp fennel seeds

15g rosemary, stalk removed and finely chopped

3 medium onions

490ml chicken stock

FOR THE BEANS

1 tbsp olive oil

30g butter

2 shallots, finely chopped

2 garlic cloves, finely chopped

15g rosemary

160ml double cream

150ml chicken stock

2 tbsp flat-leaf parsley, finely chopped

3 x 400g tins cannellini beans, drained

Salt and pepper

Preheat the oven to 220°C.

For the pork belly, boil a full kettle and, once boiled, pour the water over the pork belly, skin side up. The pork needs to be held up at an angle so the water runs off the pork immediately. This helps to achieve great crackling.

Pat dry and rub both sides with the olive oil, fennel seeds and half the chopped rosemary. Sprinkle liberally with salt and pepper.

Cut the ends of each of the onions and cut in half, lay them on the bottom of a roasting tray to create a trivet for the meat. This will stop the bottom of the meat burning and will also give the sauce a lovely flavour.

Roast the pork for 20 minutes. Remove from the oven and add 240ml of the chicken stock, return back to the oven for a further 20 minutes before adding another 240ml chicken stock. At this point the skin should have blistered evenly to give a great crackling. If the crackling isn't ready, return to the oven for a further 20 minutes.

Then turn the oven down to 135°C, add 10ml of chicken stock and roast for 2½ hours. Check the pork every 20 minutes and top up with water if the stock dries out.

Once cooked, remove the pork from the tray and allow to rest for 15 minutes.

While the pan juices are still warm, scrape the pan to release all the flavour and strain the juices into a small saucepan. Bring to the heat and reduce a little, being careful not to add any seasoning as the pan juices have reduced a lot during cooking. Set aside until serving.

Meanwhile, to prepare the beans, put the olive oil and butter into a saucepan on a medium heat and once bubbling, add the shallots and saute for 3 minutes or until softened.

When the shallots are soft, add the garlic and cook for a further two minutes before adding chopped rosemary, stir briefly and add the cream and remaining 150ml of chicken stock. Bring to the boil and reduce the heat and allow the sauce to reduce by a third. Add the beans and stir to warm through. Season and stir through the flat-leaf parsley. Keep warm until needed.

Cut the pork into six even pieces, keeping the crackling intact. The easiest way to do this is with a serrated knife, skin side down.

Serve the beans first, top with a piece of pork and drizzle with the pan juices.

conversion tables

temperature

CELSIUS	FARENHEIT	GAS	DESCRIPTION
110	225	¼	Cool
120	250	½	Cool
140	275	1	Very low
150	300	2	Very low
160	325	3	Very low
170	325	3	Moderate
180	350	4	Moderate
190	375	5	Moderately hot
200	400	6	Hot
220	425	7	Hot
230	450	8	Very hot

volume

METRIC	IMPERIAL
25 ml	1 fl oz
50 ml	2 fl oz
75 ml	2 ½ fl oz
100 ml	3 ½ fl oz
125 ml	4 fl oz
150 ml	5 fl oz / ¼ pint
175 ml	6 fl oz
200 ml	7 fl oz / 1/3 pint
225 ml	8 fl oz
250 ml	9 fl oz
300 ml	10 fl oz / ½ pint
350 ml	12 fl oz
400 ml	14 fl oz
425 ml	15 fl oz / ¾ pint
450 ml	16 fl oz
500 ml	18 fl oz
568 ml	20 fl oz / 1 pint
600 ml	1 pint
700 ml	1 ¼ pints
850 ml	1 ½ pints
1 litre	1 ¾ pints
1.2 litres	2 pints
1.3 litres	2 ¼ pints
1.4 litres	2 ½ pints
1.5 litres	2 ¾ pints
1.7 litres	3 pints
2 litres	3 ½ pints
2.5 litres	4 ½ pints

weight

METRIC	IMPERIAL	METRIC	IMPERIAL
5 g	1/8 oz	325 g	11 ½ oz
10 g	¼ oz	350 g	12 oz
15 g	½ oz	375 g	13 oz
20 g	¾ oz	400 g	14 oz
25 g	1 oz	425 g	15 oz
35 g	1 ¼ oz	450 g	1 lb
40 g	1 ½ oz	500 g	1 lb 2 oz
50 g	1 ¾ oz	550 g	1 lb 4 oz
55 g	2 oz	600 g	1 lb 5 oz
60 g	2 ¼ oz	650 g	1 lb 7 oz
70 g	2 ½ oz	700 g	1 lb 9 oz
75 g	2 ¾ oz	750 g	1 lb 10 oz
85 g	3 oz	800 g	1 lb 12 oz
90 g	3 ¼ oz	850 g	1 lb 14 oz
100 g	3 ½ oz	900 g	2 lb
115 g	4 oz	950 g	2 lb 2 oz
125 g	4 ½ oz	1 kg	2 lb 4 oz
140 g	5 oz	1.25 kg	2 lb 12 oz
150 g	5 ½ oz	1.3 kg	3 lb
175 g	6 oz	1.5 kg	3 lb 5 oz
200 g	7 oz	1.6 kg	3 lb 8 oz
225 g	8 oz	1.8 kg	4 lb
250 g	9 oz	2 kg	4 lb 8 oz
275 g	9 ¾ oz	2.25 kg	5 lb
280 g	10 oz	2.5 kg	5 lb 8 oz
300 g	10 ½ oz	2.7 kg	6 lb
315 g	11 oz	3 kg	6 lb 8 oz

linear measurements

METRIC	IMPERIAL	METRIC	IMPERIAL
2 mm	1/16 in	17 cm	6 ½ in
3 mm	1/8 in	18 cm	7 in
5 mm	¼ in	19 cm	7 ½ in
8 mm	1/8 in	20 cm	8 in
10mm/1cm	½ in	22 cm	8 ½ in
1.5 cm	5/8 in	23 cm	9 in
2 cm	¼ in	24 cm	9 ½ in
2.5 cm	1 in	25 cm	10 in
3 cm	1 ¼ in	26 cm	10 ½ in
4 cm	1 ½ in	27 cm	10 ¾ in
4.5 cm	1 ¾ in	28 cm	11 in
5 cm	2 in	29 cm	11 ½ in
5.5 cm	2 ¼ in	30 cm	12 in
6 cm	2 ½ in	31 cm	12 ½ in
7 cm	2 ¾ in	33 cm	13 in
7.5 cm	3 in	34 cm	13 ½ in
8 cm	3 ¼ in	35 cm	14 in
9 cm	3 ½ in	37 cm	14 ½ in
9.5 cm	3 ¾ in	38 cm	15 in
10 cm	4 in	39 cm	15 ½ in
11 cm	4 ¼ in	40 cm	16 in
12 cm	4 ½ in	42 cm	16 ½ in
12.5 cm	4 ¾ in	43 cm	17 cm
13 cm	5 in	44 cm	17 ½ in
14 cm	5 ½ in	46 cm	18 in
15 cm	6 in	48 cm	19 in
16 cm	6 ¼ in	50 cm	20 in

Thank You...

All my family and friends for their continued love and support

Nicole, thank you, thank you, being a wonderful friend and starting me on this journey, and thumbs up to you and Andy for introducing me to the Food Network

The Food Network UK family, particularly Nick and Sue, for encouraging me, believing in me, and investing in me. It has been a great adventure so far and I love working with such a dedicated team. (A special thank you to Heather who made this cookbook happen - sorry to drive you mad with recipes, imagery and edits)

The team at Sweet TV for making Street Feasts (big shout to the 'Brotherhood' for our 'tours of duty')

My director Ben Cole for not listening to me and making me a presenter.

James Mclean for teaching me to cook

FoodClub for continually making food fun and not just work (seven years guys!)

Matt Reuther for telling me 'Don't get caught out!'

Ania Sowinski who introduced me to Nicole

Everyone at 'Eat my Pies' for running the ship while I'm gallivanting around the world

All the food friends around the world who have inspired me on my travels and helped make my book and the Street Feasts series a success

To Alison, Hazel, Bob and everyone at Accent Press for producing this book

index